Pra...
THE BONFI

C000178623

"Trust me when I tell you that this book is unlike anything else you have read before. The conversations between Matthew and Michael recorded here range from deeply profound to hilariously irreverent, with a few dick jokes sprinkled along the path. But you'll find yourself wishing you could pull up a chair and warm yourself next to this bonfire where bullshit is eternally condemned and simple truth refined until it becomes the purest gold. Worth every penny."

— **Keith Giles**, author of the *Jesus Un* series and
cohost of the Heretic Happy Hour podcast

"Vulnerable. Refreshing. Relatable. Three words that describe Matthew and Michael's newest book. While vulnerable throughout, this book carries with it a balance in perspective which leads the reader to come to their own conclusions. This book is funny in parts while daring to ask hard questions in others. It boldly demonstrates nuance interspersed with humor and vulnerability."

— **Seth Showalter**, MHA, LCSW, Clinical Trainer
and host of the Mental Podcast

"Reading *The Bonfire Sessions: A Year of Shadow and Flame* is like sitting down with two of your most brilliant friends who invite you into their most unguarded conversations about God, faith, and the human experience. Don't miss this opportunity to walk with two mystics on the road away from certainty as they journey toward a more love-centered life."

— **Jason Elam**, columnist for Patheos and host
of The Messy Spirituality Podcast

"There is a proverb that says conversation is food for the soul! I personally believe conversation is the answer to much of the world's issues. While the theme of this book revolves around a bonfire, drinking whiskey, and working through diverse and difficult subject matter, it does so in a way that also answers many of humanity's issues. Grab a glass, take a seat, and treat yourself to a great conversation. Your soul will thank you!"

– **Michelle Collins**, heretic, gym rat, and all-around badass

"Matthew and Michael cover a wide variety of topics in this book. Their language is adult like the beverages they consume as they talk. The topics cover such things as suffering and their individual faith journeys. Because they are not trying to necessarily convince each other of anything, it is just a beautiful transparent journey between two great people."

– **Karl Forehand**, author of *Apparent Faith* and *The Tea Shop*

"In the midst of fake news, scripted reality TV shows, and deep fakes, Matthew J. Distefano and Michael Machuga's *The Bonfire Sessions* is as authentic and real as it gets. I appreciate their down to earth conversations that are beautifully raw and filled with plenty of wisdom about life, God, theology, mental health, tragedy, and everything in between. This is a great book to pick up to learn, grow, and get a rare glimpse into what true friendship and intimacy looks like."

– **Mark Karris**, licensed therapist and author of *Religious Refugees: Deconstructing Toward Spiritual and Emotional Healing*

To Speri, Lyndsay, and Elyse

First Edition

Cover design and layout by Rafael Polendo (polendo.net)

Scripture quotations, unless otherwise noted, taken from the *New Revised Standard Version* and are copyright © 1989 by the Division of Christian Education of the National Council of Churches of Christ in the U.S.A. and are used by permission.

ISBN 978-1-938480-79-9

This volume is printed on acid free paper and meets ANSI Z39.48 standards. Printed in the United States of America

Published by Quoir
Oak Glen, California

www.quoir.com

The

BONFIRE
SESSIONS

A Year of Shadow and Flame

MATTHEW J. DISTEFANO
AND MICHAEL MACHUGA

TABLE OF CONTENTS

FOREWORD

Imagine two guys with differing theological and philosophical perspectives having a discussion. Then, imagine these gents having this discussion under the stars, immersed in the beauty of nature. Now imagine these same fellows enjoying the discussion with the stimulation of cocktails and cannabis. Then imagine all of the above but add a rollercoaster—and it's on fire!

Welcome to *The Bonfire Sessions*.

In this book, the authors make the reader a "fly on the wall" for some very intimate conversations.

There's an old joke about a priest, a rabbi, and a Baptist. Well, imagine if one of the players in the joke is a Girardian theologian and the other is a Zen Buddhist. But both are universalist in their respective spiritual bent. And they're drinking adult beverages. And smoking weed! This book is a humorous, serious, devout, and irreverent deconstruction-to-reconstruction stream of consciousness.

Theology. Politics. Philosophy. Oh my!

Just like there are seasons in nature, there are seasons in life. In this book, Michael and Matthew take us through a full solar evolution of talks.

In the spring, they talk about rebirth. Michael's accident and subsequent rehab sets the stage for a range of conversations that immerse the reader in Phoenix-like, "up from the ashes" discussions. The fire, here, is one of warmth but also one of hope. Both

Michael and Matthew have some serious "life from death" experiences that they share with humor, candor, and raw emotion.

In summer, the stage is set by the aftermath of the destruction wrought by the California wildfires. Conversations about depression and anxiety give way to being in the moment and learning how to "chill" in the midst of adversity—because summer is the season of "laid back and relaxed." The bonfire here is a bit of a luxury.

In autumn and winter, the change of the seasons to a time of dying is the theme. It's not a macabre discussion, just very matter-of-fact. Here, Michael and Matthew juxtapose the dying of the leaves with the transition of some loved one's lives. In these seasons, the authors also take a deep dive into race and racism that is not only eye-opening but truly optimistic. The fire during these seasons is a necessity because it gives life-sustaining warmth in the midst of the cold reality of a time of dying.

I love how the conversations fluidly and seamlessly transition from wide-ranging topics such as depression and anxiety, "pussy-grabbing" narcissism, firearms, to how drug offenders are imprisoned (and should be released).

The most valuable takeaway from this book has been getting to know Michael (sorry, Matt). As a cohost of the Heretic Happy Hour podcast, I get to spend copious amounts of time with Matt. We have each been a guest on each other's podcasts. Matt's book *Heretic!* was a theological game changer for me. Additionally, we have a true friendship outside our electronic relationship.

Through *The Bonfire Sessions*, though, I feel like I've been blessed with the opportunity to make a new friend and commune with another like mind and spirit.

I am truly awed by the spiritual and theological range of both of these brilliant minds. This book not only has shown the strengths and vulnerabilities of both authors but also invites the reader into the conversation. These conversations take the readers on a seriously unpredictable emotional, spiritual, and intellectual thrill-ride.

This book goes from the profound to the profane and back quicker and more gracefully than a supercar goes from 0–100 miles per hour.

Most importantly, this is a true tome for the times. In spite of all the death, doom, and despair that seems to face our world, Michael and Matthew tackle many issues head on—unafraid and unashamed to introduce their own personal interpretations—and leave the reader with a sense of both optimism and hope.

While I wouldn't call this book a necessity (wait, hold your torches and pitchforks), it is a rich, high-performing, decadent *luxury*. Not everyone gets the experience of a Ferrari or Rolls Royce, but everyone who does experience them has their life paradigm changed because of the experience.

So, get in, sit down, buckle up, and hold on!

—Derrick Day
Cohost of the Heretic Happy Hour podcast
and author of *Deconstructing Religion*

PREFACE

Welcome to *The Bonfire Sessions: A Year of Shadow and Flame*. We are so glad you've decided to join us on this intimate, bromantic journey. A word of caution, however (as if we need to tell you by now): we tend to burn the midnight oil, so please first grab a comfy seat, cozy up near the fire, fill your wine glass and your hand-carved pipe, and take it all in.

As you can see, we *had* a beautiful setting here in the Sierra Nevada foothills, and I say "had" because, if you aren't aware (but as we will discuss in our Summer session), the infamous Camp Fire wiped out just about everything. The lovely little grove of fruit trees in the south part of the property? Gone. The vineyard? Gone. The orchard, smack-dab in the middle of the property? Gone. The garden? Gone. Even the fucking compost—all of it—gone!

What are you gonna do, though? Nothing except continue to have our bonfire chats. That, and clean the place up, which we've already started doing. The garden beds are already in place. A handful of trees are in. The vineyard is ready to rock. All we're missing is the Mallorn tree.

The Shire shall live on, my friends!

Anyway, in case you aren't yet aware, what we are going to do in these conversations will mirror what we do on The Bonfire Sessions podcast. We'll light the fire, fill our drinks and our pipes, and chat. About what? Anything. Everything. From discussions about our individual faith journeys, to conversations about theology and politics and philosophy. We'll pretty much cover it all. At times we'll be humorous, other times profound, but always with the spirit of friendship in mind. No matter what, we are friends. We may disagree at times, but that doesn't matter. First and foremost, we are human, which means that grace, understanding, and empathy are crucial in understanding one another.

Now, if you check out the Table of Contents, you'll notice that this journey is broken up into seasons. We did that on purpose. We started with spring because that's when things burst into life. Summer then brings adventure, and is also a time of harvest. Autumn is where you slow down, reflect, and prepare for winter. And finally, winter brings stillness and death—the death of this particular journey. But fear not, friends: There is always another spring just around the corner. (And yes, that means there is always room for another Bonfire Session.)

But in the meantime, please sit back, relax, pour your favorite drink, and let's get into it, shall we?

Matthew's
ACKNOWLEDGMENTS

First off, I want to thank my wonderful wife Lyndsay for being such a source of strength and encouragement. She is my rock, and without her I'd be a lost puppy in the wilderness.

As always, I have to thank Michael Machuga, the coauthor of this series of booklets and fellow host of The Bonfire Sessions podcast. He is and will always be my Samwise Gamgee.

I am indebted to everyone at Quoir Publishing and the Heretic Happy Hour podcast. Rafael, Teighlor, Jamal, and Keith (and now, Derrick and Katy)—I fucking love you all!

To everyone who was a part of the launch teams, thank you. Without your help, projects like these would probably never even get off the ground. Indeed, this truly was a team effort.

And to everyone who continues to support my work, I am reverentially grateful. Whether you support my podcasts, my blog, my books, my music, or all of the above, it matters not. Just the fact that you're willing to pay attention to my dumb ass means the world to me. Cheers, and here's to you!

Michael's
ACKNOWLEDGMENTS

I would like to thank:

Matthew Distefano for all his work editing and keeping me on task, and for being smart enough to have a decent conversation with.

Speri Machuga for thinking that I'm a sexy nerd and for making sure that I keep my day job.

Derrick Day for writing the foreword.

All anonymous editors, for proofreading and polishing the manuscript.

Quoir Publishing, for publishing.

Nobody else contributed anything of value.

Spring

··· 1 ···
TWILIGHT

Matthew: Alright, you beautiful motherfucker, let me kick this whole thing off by saying how much I enjoyed writing our first book, *A Journey with Two Mystics*. Without being too hyperbolic, I must say that it was one of the most pleasurable things I've ever done with another human being. (Sex is still number one, *#sorrynotsorry*.) I mean, how can you not enjoy four years of sitting around the bonfire with your best friend, a nice red wine, and a long-stemmed pipe full of the Southfarthing's finest?

That being said, I'm curious if this experience in any way changed you as a person: What have been some of the highs? Have you had any lows?

Michael: Well, our book, first and foremost, only confirmed and solidified my Buddhism, specifically the notion that the meaning of life is simply to experience it. You don't *really* know why you should write a book, for instance, until you write one. *Experience it.* Further, you don't understand why you should specifically coauthor a book until you do so. *Experience it.* More to the point, only you and I know what it's like to write our particular book. And only you and I truly know what we've gained for having done so. Only we *experienced* it.

The high of this experience, really, has been the feeling of accomplishing a bucket-list item. The low? Realizing how fleeting that feeling can be. Just a year after its publication and I can hardly recall the process. It's a wake-up call that a lazy-ass like myself can't rest on previous accomplishments.

Toward the end of our last journey, I said that I was ready to stop living in my head for a bit. You see, I don't think I'm an intellectual, to tell you the truth. All of my learning, now that I think about it, has been pointing toward something else, toward a liberation of some sorts. I don't care to learn for the sake of learning. I grabbed hold of Universalism, for example, because I needed to be free from the doctrine of eternal conscious torment. I grabbed hold of Zen Buddhism—quite ironically, I might add—because I realized I had forsaken the Naked Now. All of my intellectual efforts, then, have really just been an attempt at freedom, an unlearning, to lose myself in this life, in even the mundane things like video games—you know, to feel the Saturday morning joy of childhood once again.

So, that's essentially what I've been up to this past year. While you've been off becoming disgustingly successful, I've been playing a shit-ton of video games. You've probably noticed that it's been a year characterized more by unlearning than actual change. A year of rest, if you will. Simply put, our book put to rest my fears of living an honest, simple life. Now I just have to figure out what I *really* want to do, in addition to playing copious amounts of "Call of Duty."

I'm curious, though, having written a handful of books, does the experience change with each publication?

Matthew: Maybe this won't come as much of a surprise, but nothing really changes in terms of how fleeting the high you spoke of can be. Like most accomplishments in life, you do the damn thing and then move on pretty quickly.

Tell me, Mr. Buddhist: Is the high of accomplishing something really the goal, though? Of course not. The real high is *in* the experience, which may or may not lead to the accomplishment. As I've heard you put it, the point of the dance is to dance. And, call me biased, but we danced a commendable dance.

And now, here we are, tangled up in another duet. Only this time, I think things will take a different tone. The dance will have a different feel. But isn't that the sign of seasoned dancers?

Michael: Yes, I do believe it's time for something different. Our first dance was good, but it was too scripted for my taste. It smelled too much of purpose. If it's alright with you, I'd really like to just sit down and chat. We've been wandering in this world of ours for a while and I think we both have some stories to tell.

Matthew: Indeed, we do. Let's start getting into it, then. I thought perhaps we could begin by reminiscing a bit. Think back six years or so, when we first became friends. I've always found the genesis of our friendship interesting, even curious perhaps. Call it an act of divine providence, or call it coincidence, but whatever it was, it's been a huge blessing. And yet, really, it seemed to have taken a near tragedy for us to become as close as we are today.

Michael: Yeah, it totally did. Let me recall the gist of it, as best as I can.

The spring morning started out fantastically: dirt biking in the mountains with family, booze, weed, pain pills. It was also Easter Sunday. I'm not a religious man any longer, but for some reason Easter added to the experience. I figured worshipping in the mountains would be an acceptable alternative to church, but perhaps God felt differently.

Matthew: Well, that's what you get for skipping church, you heathen.

Michael: Right. I'm not exactly proud that I'm "otherwise altered" when I'm riding. But there's a spectrum, correct? From buzzed to smashed? In a way, and I only speak for myself here, but it can actually be safer to have a buzz than to be completely sober. You're more relaxed and ready to commit. We must remember the Buddhist dictum to never wobble. And, you know, my wife doesn't care, so judgers can suck it.

All that to say, I'm not sure what ultimately led to my crash. Most likely it was a simple lack of attention. I was just dicking around on the side of the road. I wasn't going any faster than, say, ten miles per hour. But, all of a sudden, my back tire caught a rut and the next thing I knew I was flying over the handlebars and doing a belly flop on the rock-hard ground.

I was surprised how a place that had once been heaven could so quickly turn ominous. I swear, the sky instantly went dark. I guess pissing blood does that—pissing blood and unimaginable gut pain that wouldn't go away or even lessen. I couldn't catch my breath. The funny thing is that it apparently didn't look that bad, just kinda comical. My brother-in-law was actually getting irritated that it was taking me so long to recover.

So, eventually, realizing nothing was going to get better, I got on my bike in hopes that I could get the hell out of there. It wasn't long until it dawned on me how incredibly fucked I was. I just couldn't do it. I was riding off-road and every jolt was agony. My brother and father-in-law were going to have to ride back to get the truck. That left my wife and I alone—alone in the mountains.

At the time, I don't remember my wife being that concerned. That would happen later. I didn't think I was going to die, but I knew there was no hope of relief for at least another three hours, until we got to the emergency room. I'm not good at communicating when I'm in pain so I wasn't able to convey what I was feeling. So, I don't judge her semi-nonchalance. I just felt especially alone, in the mountains, and it was starting to get dark.

Then it happened. The sound of a diesel engine could be heard approaching. The feeling was indescribable. Salvation. But if nothing else, I'd be inside, shielded from that now horrifying place. True relief, however, was hours off. Every bump in the road was, again, pure agony. Moaning was my only way to cope.

I was admitted to Feather River Hospital, only to learn that they didn't take trauma victims. So, I was put into an ambulance and got a ride to Chico, California's Enloe Medical Center. Yay! More bumps. And more encounters with a shocking lack of concern. In twenty minutes, my wife would be told by the trauma doctors to prepare herself for my death, and these guys in the back of the ambulance were acting like they were delivering a fucking pizza.

And more than that! I was still very much in the dark of night, my friend. Dawn was a way off. Just some of the highlights: my favorite sweatshirt had yet to be destroyed so that it could be removed, a tube still had to be jammed up my dick, and I still had to develop a blood clot in my lungs. I was in and out of the hospital three times in three weeks before all this shit could get sorted out.

And that's about where you come in.

It was toward the end of my stay at the hospital and my wife was reading me something that you posted on Facebook. This was April 20, 2014—4/20, y'all!—so it was back in your angry, anarchist days. I don't remember what we ended up chatting about, but I can recall it being a spirited debate, and I remember thinking that I had finally found a worthy intellectual foe—even if I didn't agree with you about much.

A couple weeks went by, I'm out of the hospital, and I remember you posted something about how evil Oxycontin is. I posted that it is better to put it in a hacky sack than in the stomach, and that weed was the only thing that helped my gut. My wife didn't like that. But you said that we should hang out sometime. Yada, yada, yada ... here we are, six years later.

Matthew: Okay, so, yeah, I remember those times. I remember being a bit of a dick now and again, even a verifiable asshole on my worst days.

Michael: I mean, your words, not mine. So, what was going on with you? I'm not sure you've ever really told me.

Matthew: Well, I suppose the best way to tackle this is to start from the beginning. It will help explain why I was so pissed-off toward the end of my 20s and then into my early 30s.

You see, the worldview that was handed to me by my parents—who, in all reality, had it handed to them by their clergy—was goddamn terrifying. It was a world in which most of those

I loved would one day fry in an eternal torture chamber called "hell," a world where demons were lurking around every corner, ready to jump into human bodies at a moment's notice, a world, in essence, that could not be trusted. I know you know what I'm talking about.

Michael: Indeed, I do. We grew up in the same CMA church, after all.

Matthew: Yeah, don't remind me.

Anyway, this worldview quickly corrupted my mind and broke my heart to pieces. To alleviate the madness, I did what any sane child would do—I tried to figure a way out. Jesus, I was told, was that way out. Done. Believe in Jesus? Of course! What nine year-old child wouldn't, given that the alternative was, without a doubt, pure, unadulterated, objective horror?

And yet, for a litany of reasons, I never actually felt secure in my faith. *What did believing in Jesus really mean, anyway?* I often wondered. Was I supposed to simply believe that Jesus was who he said he was and then go about being a normal, American kid? Or, did I have to believe and follow his teachings—teachings, mind you, that seemed out-and-out impossible? I mean, even his disciples couldn't follow him when it counted most. Think about it … it's true.

As time went on, things only got worse. Sure, on the outside, I was just fine. Internally, however, I was so fixated on death and the hellacious afterlife that could possibly be awaiting me that it drove me absolutely insane. Perhaps that is why I had so many nightmares growing up—nightmares that included run-ins with the very creatures of Dante's hell and battles on the

25

killing fields of Armageddon. And the sleep paralysis! My God, the sleep paralysis!

Needless to say, by the time I reached my later teenage years, I was pretty much a wreck. Not many people knew this about me, though. And really, they shouldn't have been expected to. I hid things fairly well, never quite making it known just how fucking petrified I was about going to hell. And if not me, then I was certainly convinced all the "non-believers" I loved definitely were.

My grandfather? Check.

My friend, Ryan, who died tragically in an auto accident? Check.

Two of my former classmates who committed suicide? Check.

All of them, bound for the abyss. And why? Because they did not say the magical salvific phrase Christians were using to get themselves into God's afterparty in the sky. This was, again, beyond horrifying and there was not a damn thing I could do about it. After all, the Bible was clear.

Until it wasn't.

As these things are wont to do, after some time—toward the end of my 20s, I think—I simply couldn't bring myself to believe this shit any longer. Sure, the God who seemed to get off on genocide and everlasting punishment was who I was told ran the world, but he had also become the one I could no longer bring myself to worship. I tried and I failed. Hard. While most of my family, friends, and pastors seemed content to sing praises to this Jason-esque deity, I was not. I could not. It had become physically impossible and no matter how many of the motions I went through, no matter how many Sunday nights I spent leading others in worship, no matter how much I read my Bible, it was literally impossible to sincerely worship this "God."

That is why—as you rightly pointed out earlier—I became so angry. I felt lied to. I felt betrayed. I felt deceived six ways from Sunday. Isolated. Alone. And so, for the better part of two years, I straddled what was, for me, the uncomfortable fence between agnosticism and atheism, where my more atheistic days were my more cynical. These were the days where I would figuratively shake my fist toward the sky—to a God I didn't even really believe in any longer—and mockingly ask how he could allow us to live in such a fucked-up world while he silently stood by, twiddling his thumbs like an apathetic moron.

Michael: Well I'll be damned! Those are some striking images. No wonder you get so much shit on Facebook. Now, tell me, do you remember your turning point? Because, I know you aren't in that same headspace any longer. I know you aren't this angry.

Matthew: No, I'm not. Thank God! Now, let's see ... my turning point? That's a tough one.

Michael: How so?

Matthew: Well, if I told you that my faith changed overnight, I would be lying. It would probably make for an intriguing story—something similar to Paul's Damascus Road event—but it would ultimately be false. I simply had too much to dig through, too much to learn—or, rather, unlearn. Plus, I still had so many open wounds from all the psychological and spiritual harm my former beliefs inflicted upon me that it was going to be impossible to discover immediate healing.

27

At the same time, though, I also had the innate drive to dig for the truth, for God (should God actually exist). I had, for whatever reason, a deep-seated desire to know what this world was all about. And I was going to stop at *nothing* to get there.

Michael: Sorry to cut you off, but, yeah, you certainly have that type of intense personality, as introverted as you *say* you are.

Matthew: Oh, I know! When I get going, I sort of get obsessed. Maybe it's my O.C.D, I'm not sure.

The cool thing is, when I dug into all this shit, I came across folks who also dug—folks like Thomas Talbott and Eric Reitan—you know, the same guys it turns out you were reading—who were, with one voice, all saying something that finally resonated throughout the whole of my being. Are you ready for it? They were all saying how God is all-loving, that God is all-merciful, that God is all-gracious, that God is all-reconciling, and that because of this, humanity would one day all live together, universally redeemed and reconciled.

Eureka!

Finally, some fucking Good News!

This was dumbfounding but true nonetheless. And it helped bring about some significant healing. Truth be told, however, none of my intellectualizing healed me as much as stumbling into your life. Correct thinking was important, sure. My brain needed it. But finding a true compatriot such as yourself was what I really needed in order for my heart and soul to discover a sense of rest, a sense of belonging. And if I may be so bold, this was salvific, for without it, the dread and horror of feeling so alone may have completely destroyed me. In other words, as it was for those in Narnia, I would have been trapped indefinitely in the throngs of winter.

Michael: Right?! I don't think I've specifically thought much of how the feeling of loneliness relates to our beliefs. I guess if I were honest, I'd have to admit that from the time of my conversion till now, I *have* felt lonely working at the church you and I grew up in, mainly because it's a place that is explicitly *against* my beliefs. Its entire business model is based on saving people from eternal conscious torment, and I just don't believe that shit any longer. Ugh! And it's always in my face, too; with all the Bible studies—or, what you like to call "The Pooling of Ignorance Sessions"—the posters, and the stupid tracts. On the other hand, if I were working somewhere secular—say, at Sierra Nevada Brewery—then perhaps I'd still be just as lonely, given that the people around me might not even believe in God. Essentially, what I'm saying is this: I've been grateful to have found someone I can relate to, someone I can hate the church with, among other shared interests.

Matthew: Well, to be fair, I don't really hate the church. I think I used to, but not anymore. That conversation, however, is going to have to wait. The grapes need watering, and I've gotta take a leak.

Be right back.

...2...
DUSK

Michael: Isn't that an amazing view from the piss-tree, looking back on the fire, with the full moon and what not?

Matthew: As close to Shire-like as I could ever imagine. Especially now that fruit trees are blossoming and the yellow roses are shining in all their glory.

Michael: You know, I think it's funny that we met after both experiencing a type of hell—the dawn after a very dark night, if you will. Mine a physical hell, yours emotional. I'm liking the symbolism.

Matthew: Funny now, but not so much then. That's the thing about good stories, though; there needs to be some drama. There needs to be a changing of the seasons; a time of death, sure, but also a time of rebirth. Without the need to go to Mordor, for instance, Frodo Baggins' tale wouldn't have been nearly as interesting. It would have basically been a story about how a Hobbit grew vegetables in the Shire. Charming, no doubt. But not *The Lord of the Rings*.

Same thing with our journeys of faith and friendship. There have been some rocky times, some moments of peril and loss, but all in all they have been completely worth it. And if neither of us had gone through the hells we went through, perhaps we would have never had the pleasure of each other's splendid company. Perhaps we would have stayed trapped in the throngs of winter.

That's the thing about hell, though. It does seem to serve a purpose. In your case, it was a hell of needing to have your broken body mended in the hospital that led you in my direction. In my case, it was a hell of having my worldview yanked from me that led me to be such a loudmouth on Facebook, which in turn piqued your curiosity about me. Strange world we live in, am I right?

Michael: I would agree that drama makes for a good story, but life is life; it's much more than a story. And I don't really like drama in real life. I'll exert an absurd amount of energy to avoid it, in fact. I mean, God can work all things for the good, sure, but I don't think that means we should go around creating drama just so we can have an adventure (or even sell some books). I guess what I'm saying is that while it puts a smile on my face to think of our story, I wasn't trying to create a good story at the time. I didn't fly over my handlebars on purpose, ya know?

Are we, therefore, required to make a choice? Between a pleasant life and a good story? Further, is a consistently pleasant life even workable? Would Samwise Gamgee have eventually wanted to blow his brains out from all the pleasant monotony if he had stayed in his Hobbit hole and never went to Mordor? Would I eventually get bored of dirt biking if every ride went off without any hitch whatsoever?

All in all, I'm really just trying to get rid of the necessity of suffering and drama because, well, suffering sucks ass. But I'm starting to think that's not possible. What do you think?

Matthew: Indeed, suffering *does* suck ass ... and not in a sexy or kinky kind of way! Having the inability to control the situation can be a bitch. However, this is the reality we all have to deal with. I don't have to tell you this, but the Four Noble Truths of Buddhism are all about suffering: the truth that it exists, the truth of what causes it, the truth of its finality, and the truth of the path that leads to its end. Plus, to paraphrase something Fr. Richard Rohr once rightly said about the matter, suffering is the best way to trust and give up control to God.[1] As I've reflected on life, this seems to be true. So, I suppose the question raised is, "What are we to do about it?"

Michael: Got any ideas?

Matthew: Well, it's my contention that we must live within the tension of the paradox. God is good in all times and in all ways— at least, that's what I hold to be true—but evil and suffering still exist. Therefore, the only appropriate thing to do, in my estimations, is to work toward the good thereby eliminating suffering wherever and whenever we come across it. I believe this was a major part of Jesus' journey in life. Quite possibly the Buddha's as well. In fact, it seems to be the focus of many of the world's great spiritual mystics.

....

1. Rohr, Richard. "Transforming Our Pain." *Center for Action and Contemplation.* (26 February 2016), para. 3. https://cac.org/transforming-our-pain-2016-02-26/.

So, given the choice between a pleasant life and a good story, I guess I'd have to go with the former over the latter. But I don't get that choice. We don't get that choice. Not all the time at least. All we can do is try to make our lives and the lives of those around us more pleasant, more joyous, more enriched, and then, if we desire to do so, tell a really good story about it.

Michael: Yeah, that sounds about right. It might also be helpful to meditate on the finiteness of suffering, to not make it more than it really is. Then, of course, as any good Buddhist would tell you, go meditate some more. And be in the moment, damnit. Chances are, the present moment isn't as bad as you might have originally thought.

I think *that* helps in most situations. Intense physical suffering will always be difficult, no doubt, but I have it on good authority that meditation still works. I cannot *fully* verify that, however, as I wasn't the Buddha that I am today back when I crashed my dirt bike. In fact—and I think my wife can verify this—I cried like a little bitch.

Matthew: Don't be so hard on yourself. I'm fairly convinced that, in one way or another, everything belongs. Plus, we all respond to pain and suffering in different ways, and whether we take things on the chin like champion boxers or whether we crumple under the force of the blows, there is always grace. Achieving Buddhahood or Christlikeness is rarely (if ever?) something that happens overnight. It's all a process, a journey, a sojourning through the deserts of doubt, insecurity, and oftentimes, fear. And there's still grace for *that*.

I think you are right, though: It *is* helpful to realize that suffering is finite. Now, I know our Christian friends will disagree with us there; you know, given the fact that they are so *certain* that some—in truth, most—will one day be lost forever to the flames of an eternal hell. But, if I may speak frankly, I don't really give two shits about their point of view any longer. "You do you, boo" is pretty much my stance these days.

As for me, I'm going to stick to the hope that suffering ends. Not just for me. Not just for my tribe. Not just for the "good Christians" of the world. But all suffering. Full stop. Truly, it's the only way for me to reconcile a good God with the overabundance of evil that pervades our world.

Michael: That makes sense to me. But people can be so certain, can't they? Certain that there is no hope—no hope for the "lost" anyway. That's one of the crucial tenets of all fire and brimstone Christians.

Matthew: Right? And isn't it funny how they are always certain they're not among the "lost," too?

Michael: Not surprising, really. Let me ask you this, though: Is certainty always a bad thing? In a way, I'm certain that all will be saved, that the universe is ultimately safe. It's nothing I can put into words though. It's not based on any deductive argument of any kind. It's an intuitive thing, one drawn from direct experience. I experience it when I hang out with you, or my wife, and, if I'm paying attention, the whole of humanity. It's the experience of love, if you want to label it. It is the experience of God *as* love, and this experience makes it crystal clear that God is not violent and could never damn anyone to hell for all eternity.

Matthew: Well, to answer your question, no, I don't think certainty is necessarily a bad thing. My problem with it, though, isn't that it's bad, but, rather, that it is an absurd notion. In other words, I think it may be impossible to be certain of anything (even, quite paradoxically, this very sentence). Convinced? Of course. But certain? I'm not so sure.

Am I just quibbling here? Maybe. But the way I see it, direct experience—completely void of all concepts and labels—while being the spice of life, makes the concept of certainty an impossible notion. It's certainly impossible to fully convey everything about a direct experience. Sure, we can talk about our life experiences till we're blue in the face, but can we ever talk about them without the grids and filters—grids and filters, mind you, that are based on anything but certainty—that shape our egos? Are we not constantly interpreting our direct experiences the moment we experience them? Hence, can we ever really be certain that we are correctly interpreting these experiences?

That is why, for me, it's best to start, not with certainty, but with trust. Trust that God is good. Trust that you are known by God. And trust that all things will work toward the good and that, in the end, nothing of value will ever be completely lost. Can we be certain of this? I don't know, but I'd have to guess not. For me, though, hope and trust in a good God is not something I need to be certain of, so I suppose it really doesn't matter.

Michael: You would definitely be in the minority here. I feel as if people—especially those fire and brimstone Christians—*need* to be certain that they're safe and loved in order to feel as if they are properly functioning humans.

Matthew: Are those types of Christians—the fundamentalist type—really functioning all that well, though?

Michael: Exactly. That's what I was getting at. I don't think fundamentalists are fully functioning humans. You see, people need some sort of adventure in order to truly live. They need a journey *and* a mystery. Fire and brimstone Christians seem to have none of that. And they seem dead inside. Might I suggest, then, that a life full of certainty is essentially dead? A non-living? A statue of the real thing?

Matthew: When I was in the throngs of that world, that seemed to be the case.

Michael: So, essentially, I feel like people need balance. People need a home *and* an adventure. Whatever you want to call it— trust, hope, certainty—people need some degree of assurance that they won't be obliterated entirely. They need to know that even if the adventures of life go awry, they can always regroup around the firepit at home, so to speak.

This is assuming that humanity—and each individual soul— is meant to exist for time-everlasting. If we exist for only a finite period, balance doesn't seem to matter. Just relax and party at home, if that's your thing; after you die, you won't exist to regret having no adventures.

Matthew: I think you are definitely onto something when you suggest that people need a degree of assurance that they won't be obliterated, that life extends past our deaths and then on into the forever. If you recall, this is something I discuss at length in my book *From the Blood of Abel*. I won't get into it too much here, but it certainly seems to be the case that human beings are neurotically afraid of death and will do anything necessary in order to experience this life as if death will never come.

Is this a bad thing, though? Not necessarily. You and I both believe that some sort of Universalism is true, and, as we've discussed around many a bonfire, that it helps aid us in the present moment. But so many times people exchange the reality of the present moment for the speculative future afterlife that they miss out on life here and now. This is tragic and is, again, a form of non-living.

But those days of non-living are well behind us, my friend. Spending twenty-five years trapped in a toxic world of "don't do this, don't do that, or you'll get zapped" was long enough. I sort of feel bad for the poor motherfuckers who are still in that world. Don't you?

Michael: I do feel bad. Looking back, that really was a terrible, inauthentic way to live. And yes, I think I can honestly say those days you just spoke of are behind me. The pendulum might have swung a little too far in the opposite direction, if I'm honest, and if you catch my meaning: I probably do swear, drink, and smoke "too much." But, at least I feel as if I'm living like a human being, and not some sort of angel/human hybrid. I still get anxious about death and what's on the other side, but that's only because it's an unknown, not because I'm worried about where I might be going. In other words, I wouldn't say I'm terrified. I know that God is good.

Matthew: Indeed, God is. At least, I hope he is. If not, then I'm afraid that all the cussing, boozing, and toking are going to bite us in the ass when it's all said and done. I mean, if our detractors are correct—if God is even close to as big a dick as most Christians say he is—then we are utterly fucked, my friend.

This, however, simply can't be. At least, I can't believe that. As we just talked about, while I'm not convinced that we can be certain of anything, it seems beyond ridiculous to think God is like the fundamentalists say. I mean, doesn't it seem as if the most likely scenario is that all fire and brimstone Christians are just projecting themselves onto the divine? That is, all this talk of wrath and judgment and hellfire are but projections of people's own internal fears and insecurities?

Regardless, what I am certain of—if we can even call it certainty—is that since leaving the world of religiosity, I've felt completely free to be myself in the here and now. You know, the only moment we truly have. Yes, I'm a bit fucked-up from time to time—more often than I'd like to admit, really—but at least I'm aware of it. At least I'm being human and not, as you so aptly noticed, some sort of angel/human hybrid. In truth, I'd rather be a hot mess than a marionette dangling from the strings of whatever church I happen to be a part of.

Michael: Haha, nice one. I think people are certainly projecting. Like I mentioned in *A Journey with Two Mystics*, and as you've stated before, nothing from reality itself—perhaps it would be better to say "concrete" reality—points to the fundamentalist worldview. Evil is born from an idea, not concrete reality. Put better yet: existence itself is not evil. If people could just chill the fuck out and get over their own minds, they'd probably see this. It's quite obvious, really. I mean, for real: we could be in a literal heaven on earth right now if people awoke to this.

Matthew: That is the tragically sad thing about the state of Christianity these days. Like I said just a moment ago, we've all but abandoned this notion that the kingdom of heaven is at-hand, that it is in our midst. Given that Jesus emphasized this all the time, it strikes me as odd that we've forgotten it. Perhaps that is what having a doctrine of eternal torment does to a person, to nearly an entire faith tradition in fact. When something as terrifying as eternal hell is potentially awaiting you—all of us, really—how could you ever truly live in the here and now? If you were on a sailboat, for example, cruising the ocean, and knew that at some point during the day a great white shark was going to devour you, would you really enjoy your excursion at sea? I highly doubt it. You'd be worried that at any moment, you'd be torn limb from limb in the most horrific of ways.

With that said, can I admit something to you?

Michael: No need to ask for my permission.

Matthew: I think all this ruminating over the afterlife has really driven me toward Buddhism. It seems much more practical. I know, I know: Jesus talked a lot about practicality—about the present moment, about being here now, about not worrying over our future, and a whole lot of other stuff about being consciously present in every waking step—but I still think

Buddhism—specifically Mahayana Buddhism—puts things in terms that I tend to find especially appealing. And more than that, this notion of the Bodhisattva resonates with me as something beautiful beyond words.

Michael: Ah! Now you're speaking my language. Tell me, what, specifically, excites you about Buddhism and the idea of the Bodhisattva?

Matthew: It just seems like the true path to being fully human. For the Bodhisattva, it's not so much about becoming enlightened for the sake of becoming enlightened, but about achieving Buddhahood for the benefit of all sentient beings. It realizes the interconnectedness of all creation, but more than that, it teaches that we are vehicles—vessels if you will—whose primary function in life is to usher in an existence void of suffering for all creatures great and small.

Now, I know what some people are going to say—that this is what Christianity is supposed to be, too. Sure. Agreed. But whereas Christianity has become so fixated on proselytizing, on converting others to their version of Jesus, on affirming this creed and that, the Bodhisattva has no such interest. For her, it's simply about living out of this place of love and compassion regardless of any conditions. Unconditional grace, if you will.

However, when it's all said and done, being the mystic that I am, I must confess that these labels—Christian and Buddhist—are irrelevant. Honestly, what is the fundamental difference between the Jesus-way and the way of the Bodhisattva? Are they both not a way of living out our true Christ/Buddha nature? Remember, in the Bible it is said that, in the end, the living

Christ will drag *all* people unto himself (John 12:32) so that *all* may see salvation (Luke 3:6). It is also said that the toil and struggle of Christians will not be in vain because their hope is in the living God, the one who is the savior of *all* people (1 Timothy 4:10). This is the way of the Christ but it is also the way of the Bodhisattva. And all we need to do to see how they are one in the same, rather than being pitted against each other—Christ vs. Buddha—is to remove our dualistic glasses and embrace the oneness of all creation.

Michael: Totally. And I think that's the crux of the matter right there. As I've made abundantly clear, I too find Buddhism more compelling, and I think it's because of the two—Christianity and Buddhism—Buddhism is more explicit about dropping labels. "Jesus." "Buddha." Same thing, really—just different contexts. But of the two, Buddhism is more overt in its practicality.

Also, since you brought it up, Buddhism is almost unambiguously anti-evangelistic. It's about the student seeking the master. The master knows that his product is the shit, the sticky-icky, and that people will naturally seek it. What's more, he knows that everybody already has the sticky-icky; they just don't know it yet. I'm reminded of Alan Watts and one of the only quotes of his I've managed to memorize: "When you confer spiritual authority on another person, you must realize that you are allowing them to pick your pocket and sell you your own watch."[2] In other words, the watch is yours already; you don't need someone to profit off giving back to you what they stole in the first place.

....

2. Watts, Alan. *Still the Mind: An Introduction to Meditation.* Novato: New World Library, 2000, 23.

Christians, then—more specifically, Evangelicals, I guess—seem to have no faith in what they're selling, as far as I can tell, and that's why all their music and literature is so—and I'm sorry to have to use his word—derivative. Unlike the Buddhist, they also have no faith that people will find their own way, always assuming that people would be completely lost without their gift to the world. It's insulting, really.

Fucking self-important assholes.

Alright, I obviously need to cool off. Be right back.

3

MIDNIGHT

Matthew: Okay, so I know we've already established that I had some anger issues in the past, with much of it directed at the evangelical church. However, it also seems safe to say that you have a little pent-up rage as well. Not that there's anything necessarily wrong with that. I mean, evangelicals can certainly be pretentious and boastful little bastards. But let's talk about that. Let's unpack some of this fire that obviously burns in your belly—if you've chilled the hell out, of course.

Michael: I hit some of that Kush you brought, so I'm good now. You know what's funny? As I was pissing and smoking, I realized how much the evangelical church reminds me of Donald Trump, in that both are loud and obnoxious and both have a tenuous relationship with truth. It's a marriage made in hell, really. And the more I think about it, the more infuriating it is to see two childhood staples—country and religion—going down the crapper. To tell you the truth, I'm embarrassed to be considered either American or Christian.

It's doubly frustrating because I don't know how to have a conversation with either evangelicals or Trump supporters (not that they are typically different). As one of my heroes, Barack Obama, once put it, we're living in two different information universes. Trump supporters have Fox News; liberals have the mainstream media. Evangelicals have only the Bible; Universalists like you and I draw on everything. Finding common ground sometimes seems too hard to even attempt and I get genuinely worried that things will never get worked out.

Matthew: Who says they need to get worked out? I mean, it's not like life is such that we all need to converse with one another. If people want to stay trapped their little bubbles, if they think that Fox News is some bastion of objective truth, or that the Bible is some divinely-written book that fell from the sky and has the answers to all of life's questions, then fuck it, let them have it. Our time is our own and it's all a zero-sum game. If we choose to spend our days conversing with myopic idiots who think Sean Hannity speaks gospel every time he opens his goddamn mouth, then that is time we are not spending with others who are more nuanced, more rational in their approach. Honestly, I only have interest in chatting with those in the latter camp these days.

But I feel you. It would be nice to be able to bridge the gap, so to speak. It would be nice to be able to sit down with evangelicals—you know, the folks we used to break bread with—for more than thirty seconds and not be told we're going to hell for rejecting their message. But alas! They seem so fucking fragile that they would rather demonize us than step outside of themselves in order to show some empathy. And look, I know that not all evangelicals are like this. I know there are some solid thinkers and other folks who will tolerate views they don't agree with. Sadly, however, they are few and far between, the exception to the rule—a rare breath of fresh air amidst the stifling toxicity that we call evangelical Christianity.

Michael: I suppose that's the beauty of Universalism, isn't it? The great thing about having a good God who's actually sovereign is that he has all the time in the world to accomplish his purposes. Protestants believe that as the tree fails, so shall it lie. But Catholics, with their purgatorial views, don't. So, even within mainstream Christianity it's hard to make the case that people have a limited time to reach the finish line. Like you said, why waste your breath on people who aren't ready to listen to anything outside their microscopic boxes? Why do *we* have to be the ones reaching out? Let them wallow in their own filth. I know that sounds fantastically arrogant, but somebody's gotta be right, and I'd rather be bold than polite.

Matthew: I don't think it sounds arrogant at all. I tend to be a bit of an arrogant asshole, though, so take from that what you will. However, we both know how much time you and I spent in that world and if experiential knowledge means anything then we both know how much wallowing indeed goes on in it. And before anyone accuses me of being an even bigger asshole for saying such a thing, I include myself first.

You see, if I'm being perfectly honest, my time in the evangelical church can probably *best* be described as wallowing. It wasn't sincere living. I, like so many others, were a part of the church because it made us feel better about ourselves. And so, we wallowed in the nostalgia of what Jesus did for us on the cross; we wallowed in being included among those who would go to heaven when we die; we wallowed in hearing our pastors tell us, over and over, what we already knew and believed (which was that *we* were the special ones included in God's blessed family). But we didn't strive toward a sort of living that was in any way authentic, lest we found ourselves *not* included in what happened at the cross, not included among those who went to heaven, and not included in God's inner circle.

After all, every last one of us—the Christians included—were filthy. I still believe this, of course, the only difference is that I admit it. That's the biggest issue I have with Christianity; they are just as fucked-up as the rest of us except they like to pretend they're not. Sure, they'll always admit that they have room to grow and that they could probably do well to sin less, but living from a place of vulnerability and nakedness is not their forte. But again, that isn't necessarily their focus. For them, it's not about an at-hand kingdom of God, it's not about contemplative living in the here and now; it's entirely about avoiding hell. Ironic, then, that it is this very way of living that creates such a place.

And look, like I just said a moment ago, I'm not suggesting that there isn't anything good about what the evangelical church does. Like most everything, it's a bit of a mixed bag. It just seems the truth of the matter is that all the good the church does could be done without all the harmful religious bullshit that comes along with it.

Michael: Um, excuse me, did you just call me filthy? I'm not sure if I should blush or be insulted. I feel we should be clear that people aren't filthy through and through. There's a thin film of filth, sure, but it can be washed off easily enough; it's nothing like Augustine's concept of original sin or any bullshit like that. And yet, if I'm honest, I would classify *much* of what goes on at church as filth: shallow songs that sound spiritual, messages from the pulpit that do nothing to help you engage the present moment, everything that you just mentioned, blah, blah,

blah. I do like the Food Pantry and the Clothes Closet ministries, though. It's hard to deny their concrete contribution (the Food Pantry, however, regrettably still feels the need to drone on about Jesus, rather than simply feeding the poor).

The bad thing about filth, of course, is that it obstructs beauty. It covers the innate sparkle and shine of the human soul, which is complete and needs no savior—no savior like the one imagined by evangelicals, I mean. I think all we need is a good janitor, really. Like Sir Lancelot, I take offense to anything—be it conceptual or concrete reality—that brings a man to his knees. All this evangelizing is giving people the wrong fucking idea. People are not worthless filth, but if you keep telling them that they are, gosh darn it, they're gonna act like it. So yes, self-fulfilling prophecies, like this morally atrocious notion of original sin (shout out to David Bentley Hart[3]), is quite ironic indeed.

Matthew: I'm glad you called me out on that shit. But let me clarify: I don't mean to say that we are filthy in the way Calvinists, for example, think of things; I'm just suggesting we all do shit that is not healthy or helpful to either ourselves or others. That said, I believe you're right; our *true essence* is not filthy at all. Made in the image of God, we are all, at our core, good. Plus, "filthy" is just a label anyway, one generally derived by whatever our culture or religion establishes for us prior to us even being born: don't fuck in this way, do it like this; don't smoke, especially weed; don't drink wine, okay, maybe just a little; don't say "shit" or "damn" or "fuck," say "shucks" or "darn"

....

3. Hart, David Bentley. "God, Creation, and Evil: The Moral Meaning of creation ex nihilo." *Radical Orthodoxy: Theology, Philosophy, Politics*, Vol. 3, Number 1 (September 2015): 6–9.

or "fiddly sticks." And at the end of the day, it's all too much to bear, really. We are adults, for God's sake, not children who need constant reminders of what *not* to do.

All this makes me think of something you rightly noted in our first book, which is that when we focus on all the things we may happen to crash into (i.e., sin), we end up slamming into the very things we had hoped to avoid. Like a squirrel who panics in the middle of the road, a mere foot from the safety of the shoulder, we spastically jolt back and forth until a semi-truck plows into us, splattering our guts across the asphalt. How many Christians have experienced something like this? I know I have.

Michael: Again, it's all just a self-fulfilling prophecy, is it not?

Matthew: Exactly. It reminds me of the time I, as an evangelical teenager, was forced to read the book *Every Young Man's Battle*. Remember that pile of shit? If you don't, allow me to remind you: essentially the author attempts to dissuade young men from lusting, looking at porn, and beating off, and he does this by basically telling them it's bad, impure, and against God's order of things. Over and over, this is emphasized. And wouldn't you know it, this sort of sexual repression didn't work (has it worked for anybody?). In fact, I only found myself lusting more, looking at more porn, and beating off so much I'm actually kinda surprised my palms remained hairless.

I don't mean to sound crass in saying that—okay, I do—but it's so true! Like you just said, if we keep hearing how fucking wretched we are then it shouldn't surprise anyone when we act accordingly. It's like parents who constantly tell their children how they are nothing but little shits, and then act all surprised when their kids become absolute monsters. If folks stopped feeding them bullshit, perhaps they'll respond in kind.

Michael: Ha! "Hairy palms." I honestly never read that book, but it sounds like it might make for some good comedy when I'm stoned out of my gourde.

I guess I have to ask, however, what's so bad about being a little shit—like, a literal little shit. A little shit smells unpleasant, but as you pointed out, couldn't that just be in the realm of a cultural norm? My dogs seem to thoroughly enjoy cat shit, for example. And seafood smells just as foul to me as refuse does but I wouldn't call it evil. For me, it's helpful to consider the Buddhist notion of direct pointing. If you can't point to something in concrete reality, how important is it? So, for instance, I would ask all these white-washed tombs to point to their righteousness, because all I see is a self-righteous smirk of derision, and I've gotta say, it's not very attractive. Or, conversely, I would ask the prostitute's accuser to point to her impurity. Where is the righteous man's purity for that matter? I'm not trying to be obtuse; I really can't find the real-world counterparts to these abstractions. Is this why were told to not judge?

Coming at it from a different angle, I think many Christians conflate righteousness with being sanitary. I'm obviously down with finely-crafted profanity, and I think women's bodies are to be celebrated (and apparently so does the Bible)—things considered by many to make one unclean. But I would ask, just to prove my point, what's worse: ogling a hottie at the supermarket or demonizing the immigrant? Looking at porn or snatching asylum seekers from their families?

Matthew: Isn't it funny how often the church emphasizes so-called "unclean" behaviors while at the same time turns a blind eye to the behaviors that actually cause the most harm in the world? I don't necessarily condone ogling hotties who are cruising around Trader Joe's—women aren't pieces of meat for goodness' sake—but you'd think that after listening to church leaders for any length of time that the worst thing we could do as humans is be un-puritanical. I mean, when's the last time you heard a sermon on opening the borders to refugees, on feeding or clothing the homeless, on counseling the drug addict or alcoholic, on disarming bombs and beating our AR-15s into plowshares, or on caring for the battered prostitute? My guess is it's been a while—or even not at all—since our focus is typically on how not to do those behaviors that we find objectionable: don't cuss, don't drink, don't smoke, don't have sex before marriage, don't beat off (or flick your bean if you're a woman), don't be gay, don't do this, don't do that, blah, blah, blah.

And look, I know we've sort of beat a dead horse but I again want to reemphasize something: it's not that Christianity is so utterly repulsive because of their so-called sin, their inability to live "clean" lives, it's that they feign sainthood, all the while living like sinners. And so, "white-washed tombs" seems entirely apropos.

To that end, if I had one final thing to say to these folks, it is this: *Y'all motherfuckers need to step up your game.*[4] Stop pretending you're something you're not. Stop acting like your shit doesn't stink. Stop worrying about what others are doing, who others are fucking, and clean up your own porch first. You shouldn't denounce my pot-smoking, for example, if you're

4. Shout out to Dave Chappelle for this phrase.

a raging alcoholic. You shouldn't denounce gay people for "ruining the sanctity of marriage" if you're on your third spouse. You shouldn't call Muslims violent when you vehemently reject a non-violent Jesus. You feel me? Step up your game. Or don't. Just don't be surprised when everyone be like "Peace out, bitches!" You really only have yourself to blame.

Michael: I feel you, but I don't quite understand how you get from point A to point B. What's the mechanism that gets you from legalism to true spirituality? I don't know, and maybe that's the point. It's not about me or "understanding." It's about being a hippie; it's about love. It's about experiencing a vision that's forced upon you. I want to understand so that I can give advice, but I'm seeing that's mainly pride speaking. In other words, I want to feel important. I get that people are the hands and feet of God, but ultimately spiritual authority lands on the individual. It all depends on what the individual chooses to accept, and who or what has control over that.

Anyway, I'm sorry but I'm super tired and am not sure if what I just said even makes sense to me. So, with that, I'm just gonna head to bed. Feel free to enjoy the fire as long as you like.

Matthew: Alrighty then. I'll watch it burn down a bit and then put it out before I leave. Goodnight, you beautiful bastard.

Summer

4

TWILIGHT

Matthew: Jesus Christ! This place looks like a warzone. I can't believe it's all gone. The house. The orchard. The garden. All of it… fucking gone.

Michael: Yep. All gone! And yet, I'm surprised how little I care. Don't get me wrong, I loved my house. I loved the layout and the fact that my wife and I designed it ourselves. I loved that it was the place you and I fire-pitted and gardened. But when I came back to the devastation a month after the fire, nary a tear came to my eye. Maybe because I didn't lose anything, really. Nobody died. We had insurance. We have a decent place to live in the interim. So, if anything, I feel liberated. Time to buy some fresh new shit!

Matthew: I must give you props for that attitude. It's not an easy one to have and is not how many have responded to this tragedy. And tragedy is what it was! Eighty-six people are dead. Over 18,000 structures are lost. 153,000 acres have been scorched. And the total cost is in the billions. But again, I love how you are approaching things. Buddhist as fuck, I'd say.

Michael: I'm pretty damn enlightened, I know.

Matthew: Yeah, yeah. We get it. Buddhism rules; Christianity sucks. Actually, now that I say that, I kinda agree. But, really, I'm not that interested in a discussion about which of these two faiths are better—that wouldn't be very enlightened, now would it? What I *am* interested in is hearing about your dramatic exit out of Paradise the morning of the fire. Based on your texts, that shit sounded horrible. But I'm sure actually being in the midst of the inferno was beyond what mere texts could convey.

Michael: Well, we woke up on that Thursday to an orange sky and ash in the trees. I could see the plume of smoke to the north, up by Concow. But, you know, it seems like Concow is burning every year. No big deal. An hour or so later at work, however, it was obvious that all was not well. The sky was dark and raining embers. We got a call on the radio at work that the mobile home park behind the building I work at was on fire. My boss and I, as well as a host of other volunteers, spent half an hour trying to keep the flames from crossing the property, and then a city official told us that we had to evacuate. By then, however, the roads were already clogged so I knew I couldn't drive home, even though I lived just a mile away. So, I grabbed a mask from the shop and ran home anyway. Literally, I ran. On foot. Through the chaos. When I got there, my wife met me at the top of our street with the truck and animals and a few other odds and ends that she had time to grab.

Trying to escape Paradise was, to quote Gandalf, all "shadow and flame." I didn't think I was gonna die, but the crazy part is that I wasn't quite sure. We hit a bottleneck at the exit out of Paradise, which forced us to say our goodbyes and prepared us to run like hell. Thankfully, before we had to do that, the bottleneck cleared, and we were on our way down the hill to Chico.

Matthew: I think that was the scariest part about this whole ordeal. Paradise was simply not set up to handle 30,000 residents. With only like three or four exits out of town, y'all seemed fucked from the get-go. How long did you have to agonizingly wait in traffic before things cleared?

Michael: It took about two hours. Traffic was surprisingly civil. I didn't see the worst of it, though, so don't normalize my experience. I got lucky.

Matthew: Yeah, based on the accounts I heard about, shit got crazy for a lot of folks. So much so, that I'd be surprised if there wasn't a book released sometime in the future, chronicling people's stories. From folks running uphill for miles to save their children to nurses delivering babies in the midst of the inferno, it sounded like an apocalyptic movie of sorts.

That's the thing about people, though. When shit hits the fan, we tend toward some pretty amazing things. What's fascinating, too, is that when tragedies like this strike, we don't care about race, religion, color, creed, and sexual orientation; we just do what we gotta do in order to help one another out. It's rather incredible, really, and just goes to show you the power of the present moment, for good or for ill.

Michael: I would say the present moment only has power for good. I can't think of any problem that is exacerbated by being in a meditative state. It's not a complete cure, though, at least not in this life. The day-to-day depression that I have to deal with completely vanished on the day of the fire, for example, but I was still scared as hell.

Matthew: Right. I suppose I should clarify what I said. I don't mean that the present moment is anything but good. It's just that sometimes we are thrust into it during powerfully good moments as well as powerfully terrifying ones. And in both instances, nothing but the moment matters. When you were fleeing from the flames, you weren't reminiscing on past events or ruminating about the future; you were simply there. Present. In the moment. There was no room for depressing thoughts about what you could have made of your life up until this point, nor for dread about what may befall you in the future. And sure, while your fight-or-flight response was kicked into overdrive, thus rendering you "scared as hell," at least you were present with it. Because let's be honest: too often we aren't present in life. We may physically be "here," but our minds are often "over there."

Michael: Word. Pardon the possible hyperbole, but I think the biggest obstacle we face is not realizing that we're always in the present moment. The biggest problem is awareness. Even if we're "in our heads," "over there," we're still "right here." We're experiencing being in our heads. We're experiencing being "over there." I don't see how that's bad. Be in your head, thinking thoughts, or be "present," no matter what you're up to. Whatever you feel like doing. The product of our minds is just as concrete as anything else in creation. So, don't wobble. Experience the experience. Just don't be deceived.

Matthew: That's the non-dual view I'm falling in love with, right there. We too often fall for the trap that it's somehow bad to be in our heads. But what if we accept the view that it's okay to be in our heads so long as we are present and aware about the whole matter? In other words, if we are reminiscing about the past or planning for the future, that's okay. Just be present with your thoughts. Like you said, don't wobble.

That being said, no matter how sacred, mundane, or profane the act, we must always be present with it. And I don't mean we simply go through the motions while our minds wander off into some nether region of time and space. I mean, we really get down to business. We are present. We are aware of each sensation. We feel ourselves feeling the situation. You know what I mean?

Michael: Yeah man; pin those ears back and dive in! There's this wonderful story of a mystic—I can't remember who, sorry—who exclaimed with joy at the moment of his enlightenment, "This is it! This is all there is!" I imagine that he was previously an anxious fellow, always worrying about the problems he'll have to deal with in the future. He then realized that when the problems of the future become the problems of the present, they somehow diminish. I think understanding that helps engage the present moment—when you don't have the weight of the future or past on your shoulders.

Matthew: That seems more than true. And plus, since we are both Universalists, what the fuck are we so worried about, really? Sometimes it annoys the bejesus out of me, given how much I still struggle with depression and anxiety. Like, chill out

61

Matthew. God is good. God will get what God wants. So, calm the hell down because in the end, everything's gonna be alright. And if it's not gonna be alright, then there really isn't a damn thing I can do about it anyway, so why worry? Either way, it would be better just to chill out and live in the present moment; whether that present moment is pure bliss or pure hell matters not because it is all we concretely have.

Michael: I'm becoming more and more convinced that anxiety is a physical problem. The times that I'm most anxious are the times I'm most physically depleted. My problems haven't gotten worse; my body has just gotten weaker. I can't remember the last time I woke up after a good night's sleep and was still anxious about something. Say I got a good night's sleep, had a monster breakfast, and rode my kickass mountain bike up to the lake and back: what are the chances I'd be anxious or depressed about something? I might recognize that I have a few problems to solve, but my body would be up to the task.

Matthew: So, in essence, set your life up in such a way that you are able to do what you want, when you want, and not what you or society thinks you *should* do. That seems like a good plan, so long as it's attainable. Bills have to be paid, and what I want to do—writing, podcasting, music-making—doesn't quite cut it yet, so "should" is still all too often my focus. But, perhaps it's all a process and I'm just not "there" yet.

Michael: I think I'm willing to label anxiety as a wasted emotion, along with embarrassment. As you say, we're Universalists, so what exactly do we have to be anxious about? Pain of death—or pain of anything, really—seems to be the most legitimate concern. I've experienced pain and it really hurts. But other than that, all other anxieties seem to be based on pride of some sort: fear of failure, etc. If you're doing something with your life that you truly enjoy, is failure or success even in your lexicon? But, of course, as you say, we live in the real world where maybe you can't immediately have your dream job. But once you do, life should, theoretically, be golden. You and the universe will be in perfect harmony.

Matthew: Most of that I can agree with. However, as someone who suffers with anxiety—as well as a good dose of depression from time to time—I'm not sure it has anything to do with pride. I think there are some biological and physiological factors at play here. Plus, much of my anxiety has nothing to do with me personally; rather, I'm often anxious over what is going to happen to others in the future. I get anxious over my daughter's safety and happiness. I get anxious over whether my wife is happy and content. Shit like that. But—and I'm speculating here—perhaps my anxiety is really driven by how *I* am going to feel if my loved ones suffer. I don't want to be too dualistic, though, because the reality is that it's probably a bit of both: my anxiety is a bit selfish and at the same time driven by a deep love for my family and friends.

Michael: Too right then. I probably did overestimate how much pride is responsible for anxiety. Damnit, now I'm embarrassed. I suppose I was thinking of anxiety as it relates to embarrassment, and I do think embarrassment is all about pride. Like, take my anxiety of having to talk to strangers on the phone. I don't do well with strangers anyway, but for some reason talking on the phone is even worse yet. I get especially lost for things to say; I get a tension in my gut, and I get really worried that I'm looking like an idiot. It's a feedback loop. If I didn't care so much about how people perceived me, then I'm pretty sure I wouldn't be such a mess.

Matthew: Yeah, I totally get that. It would be wonderful if we could just give the big middle finger to caring what others think of us, but it's damn-near impossible isn't it? I mean, it's one thing to care about what our loved ones think of us, but why do we care so much what strangers or even acquaintances think? I'm sure it has to do with fitting in with some sort of tribe or clan, and not wanting to stand out lest we find ourselves playing the role of scapegoat. But really, unless we are in immediate danger, being perceived as an idiot shouldn't really matter. You're forty and I'm nearly there, so it's probably high time we stop giving a fuck what people think of us.

Michael: And, like we've talked about several times before, it's helpful to remember that people don't think about you very much anyways. Which is good news to me, because I know that my life doesn't stand up to intense scrutiny. It probably, however, comes as a shocking blow to any narcissist.

Matthew: Does anyone's life stand up to intense scrutiny? I mean, if everyone were honest, then probably no. Every single one of us has baggage. Every single one of us have done shit we're not proud of, whether in the distant past or even five minutes ago. So, judge not, motherfuckers!

But you're right: people aren't thinking about you as often as you may initially think. Sometimes that tends to sting—like when you realize you probably aren't really crossing the minds of family and friends—but all in all, it's probably a good thing. Why? Because it means you are a little freer to do whatever the hell you want without people pining over what you're up to. Sure, people can be judgmental little pricks, but most of the time they are too worried about their own lives.

Michael: Which leads to an interesting question: what do you suppose Donald Trump really enjoys? He is obviously a narcissist and enjoys thinking that he has everyone's attention. Which he does! He has my attention more than I care to admit. But I bet it still isn't as much as he would like. What would he pursue if he realized his efforts for attention-grabbing were in vain? Barbecuing hamberders?

Or take me for example. I'd like to think that I'm not a narcissist, but I did waste a lot of time in college pursuing majors that I thought would impress other people, as opposed to ones that I truly enjoyed. But I guess everyone's on a scale. So, do what you like and judge not.

Matthew: Well, if I had to guess what Trump enjoys, I suppose I would just take him at his word and say, "grabbing pussy." Oh, and without consent. Allegedly. Now, don't get me wrong, I love pussy; I'm just a consent sort of guy. I find that to be an important component when it comes to pussy grabbing, ass grabbing, booby grabbing—all manners of grabbing, really. The more rapey-minded among us may not agree, but then again,

I've never taken advice from a tangerine-colored, overweight scumbag with bad hair; so, to each their own, I guess.

Anyway, all Trump-bashing aside, I think we all have a little narcissism in us. We all probably do shit with the sole purpose of impressing others. Our egos eat praise up like Trump eats up hamberders. So, again, stop judging others and yourself and just spend your days doing what you want. Live for a living, as my boy Jamal Jivanjee would say.

Michael: Agreed. I do think that maybe we should keep the Trump-bashing to a minimum, however. When he declares himself President for life—with the Republican party's blessing, of course—I don't think we'll find it so funny when he hauls our butts off to prison.

Matthew: Wouldn't that be the day? Hauled off to prison for making fun of someone... land of the free, am I right? It wouldn't be the first time our "great nation" did some shady shit like that, though, now would it? For now, I think we are safe. Safe enough, I suppose. I do have to take a leak and refill my cup, however, so let's pick this back up after I get back.

Michael: Yeah, that sounds good. After all that shit-talking, I need a refill, too.

··· 5 ···
DUSK

Matthew: Ah, that's better. You know, since you mentioned us being hauled off to prison for badmouthing the Tangerine King, it got me thinking: isn't it hilarious how we live in a nation that celebrates freedom—worships it, really—and yet, so many of our citizens are locked up in cages for things like smoking weed, soliciting prostitutes, and other nonviolent offenses? Who was it—Jim Jeffries, I think—that mentioned how in Amsterdam, you can be smoking weed whilst having sex with a prostitute in front of a cop, and you still wouldn't get arrested? That's not really my cup of tea, but the point is obvious: America isn't quite as free as we'd like to think. Not in any universal sense of the word, anyway.

Michael: Maybe not, but to be honest, I don't feel like my life is impeded. Like you, I don't have the urge to bang a hooker. Any drug that I would like to take is already legal in my state. All I need is my beer and my video games at the end of an honest day's work, and mountains to play in on the weekend. I'm glad that I'm not a gun nut, because I think that's a "freedom" that might need to go.

Matthew: I feel you. I just think it's quite peculiar how Americans talk so much about freedom, as if we are the only free country on God's green earth. We're not—not by a longshot. In fact, we're so unfree that we have the world's highest incarceration rate. I'm not joking; it's higher than even Russia, the Philippines, and all the other totalitarian countries out there. So, doesn't it sort of raise the question: If we are so goddamn free, why are so many of us locked up? But again, it probably comes back to guns. It's always the fucking guns for the freedom-loving folks. As if the measuring stick of freedom is the ability to brandish an AR-15 in your local Walmart. Funny, that.

Michael: I suppose that's either because policies are stupid or because we're simply a nation of dumbasses. We either get locked away for life for nonviolent crimes, for example, or we're quicker on the draw than Wild Bill Hickock. A lot of the former, and some of the latter, I'm guessing.

Matthew: You're probably right. In fact, I know you are. There are, to this day, people who are still locked up from the '70s for marijuana possession. In the freedom-loving state of Texas no less! But again, places like that aren't really interested in freedom as such. They are interested in not being taxed—which is all fine and good—as well as carrying their guns wherever they please. If they were really interested in freedom, they'd legalize drugs and let people exchange sex for money. Not really popular notions in some parts of the country, but if you wanted to be consistent, well, I think the point is obvious.

Michael: Texans, I would say, are little concerned with actual freedom, or consistency, or, apparently, reasonableness. And they're ugly: they like guns and they want to keep their guns, and have no problem hiding behind the guise of self/family protection. And they smell like cabbage.

Matthew: Careful, now! There are some badass Texans out there. To quote Michael Scott, I am Beyoncé, always. Most of the rest are probably not my cup of tea though. Seriously, though: I've never understood the rationale that in order to protect one's family, you need to own a vast array of firearms. No joke, I know a handful of folks who use the "argument" that they need an arsenal in order to defend the homestead, and in my mind I'm like, "You need 15 AR-15s in order to protect yourself? What are you waiting for, a zombie apocalypse?" It's asinine, really. On top of that, most of these folks are Christians, who apparently never heard of the verse that says, "Those who live by the sword will die by the sword." As if modern Jesus wouldn't apply the same logic to guns.

Michael: Asinine indeed. Great word. Even if I believed that gun owners solely cared about protection, I refuse to buy into that culture of fear. It's the same reason why I have such a hard time getting up in arms about immigration, even "illegal" immigration. Life is dangerous enough—what with natural disasters and disease—without dwelling on remote possibilities like getting robbed and murdered by an immigrant. It's such an exhausting way to live.

Matthew: And not to mention the fact that, statistically speaking, you have a far greater chance of getting robbed or murdered by someone born in the States than someone who immigrated here. But the conservative pundits aren't really interested in facts and data; they'd rather latch onto anecdotes so that they can push their fear-based agenda that Brown and Black people from countries they can hardly pronounce are dangerous thugs. It's pretty gross, I tell ya.

Michael: And they're pushing this fear-based agenda because they're terrified, for whatever reason, of losing the majority position in America. Is that the same thing as being racist? It sure sounds like it; but I *guess* there could be a difference between considering yourself superior and simply not caring for other races. I prefer coffee, but that doesn't mean it's inherently better than green tea.

Matthew: Having a particular taste for one product over another is one thing, but not caring for a particular race simply because they are from a different place, or have different colored skin, or speak a different language, is quite another. Plus, I'm of the mind that the best way to talk about racism is to talk about it systemically. In other words, forget for a second whether individuals are racist or not, and have the bigger conversation about whether cultural and political systems are in place that benefit one race over another. Because when we take it to the systemic level, we'll definitely notice that white folks are often given an upper hand, while Black and Brown folks tend toward having to fight an uphill battle. And so, whether we are individually racist or not doesn't quite matter as much as realizing that those of us with less melanin in our skin benefit from racist structures.

Michael: Your point being, perhaps, that racists don't exist in a vacuum? Racist people are racist because they live in a racist society. Fix the society and you necessarily fix the individual. Easy-peasy.

Matthew: God, if it were that easy! Because what we have is a bit of a conundrum: do you fix the individuals in order to fix the society or do you fix the society which then leads to fixed individuals? I'm not quite sure. Maybe it's not either/or but both/and. But whatever the solution is, we first must at least admit that many of our social systems are inherently racist. That doesn't mean that white folks won't have a tough time in life. Many will. Especially poor white folks. But it just means that their issues won't be directly related to them having lighter colored skin. That's the plight of Black and Brown folks. They are the ones who, in spite of drug use being relatively equal amongst whites and Blacks, are locked up for simple drug possession at alarmingly higher rates. They are the ones who have a harder time getting bank loans so they can purchase property. They are the ones who have to deal with having the cops called on them for barbequing at the park, or for listening to loud hip-hop in front of crotchety white people. And they are the ones having their necks pinned down to the point of death by racist fuckers who hide behind a badge. So, again, perhaps we need to work on people so that our society can break free from this, but at the same time, work on our systems so that people can start to see how fucked-up and racist they are.

Michael: I think it's certainly a both/and situation. One feeds into the other. It doesn't make sense to talk about a culture without talking about the individuals that make up that culture. In our country, white people like having the advantages of white privilege while at the same time pretending that they're smarter (i.e., better at evading the cops) and harder working (i.e. they earned their high-paying job). It's a pretty sweet gig. But we need to knock that off. Louis C.K. is of the opinion that we deserve to be gang-raped for all eternity, and I'm having a hard time disagreeing.

Matthew: Well, unless you're into that shit, that sounds like eternal conscious torment, and I just can't get down with any of that noise. But I know you're joking. Right? Please tell me I'm right.

Michael: Do you know me but at all? I feel like I've been crystal clear about my attitude towards butt-fucking: there's nothing wrong with it but it's not for me. I'm admittedly speaking from ignorance, however; it could be awesome, and I don't know what I'm missing. But I'm obviously not down with eternal conscious torment. You know that. I think the history of atrocities committed by white people is grim, though. I'm not joking about that. I think apologies are owed—perhaps at least a card and some weed.

Matthew: I'm right there with you, on the racial stuff at least. But shit... we can't even get some (most?) white people to admit there is anything to this notion of white privilege. It's like a whole host of them aren't listening to Black folks. Sort of reminds me of that scene from *Dumb and Dumber*, where Harry is trying to convince Lloyd that "you can't triple stamp a double stamp," and Lloyd sticks his fingers in his ears and is having none of it. Maybe if they got their fingers out of their ears and shut the fuck up for a few minutes, they'd be able to show just an ounce of goddamn empathy. You feel me?

Michael: I do indeed. I don't know how to make them listen though. Every seismic shift in my own thinking has come because I *wanted* to learn. But how do you make people want to learn or be empathetic? I've heard that reading novels—where you really get to see what is going on in someone else's head—helps develop an empathetic posture. But how do you make someone truly read and absorb a book? Maybe it's something that will have to wait for a person's next reincarnation, when their body is placed in a different environment.

Matthew: What you are getting at is one reason why I still think reincarnation has validity. It makes sense to my mind that the best way for the soul to travel toward empathy—and justice for that matter—is to live many different kinds of lives. So, for instance, we *all* live a life of bigotry as well as one who is oppressed by bigots. In other words, our soul tastes what it is like on the end of both spectrums in order to learn the truth of what it means to not judge. To judge and condemn another based on the color of their skin, their sexual orientation, their gender, their faith tradition, etc., is to judge and condemn one's self... literally. I know this isn't the only way it needs to work, but it at least makes sense to me that it could work in this manner.

Michael: The problem with that model, of course, is that hating on someone like Donald Trump no longer makes me feel better about myself. But the flipside is not feeling shame in the presence of a Saint Francis or Ronan Farrow. It's ultimately a

75

liberating realization, something useful to meditate on if you're looking to kill the ego and live freely in the present moment.

Matthew: I'm not sure killing the ego is really all that useful, though. I mean, everything belongs, right? Even the ego? Maybe the ego doesn't need to be killed; it just needs to shut the fuck up most of the time. At the same time, don't we need the ego to talk to one another? Or, perhaps I'm way off and these couple of sentences are proof that my ego needs to die a quick and sudden death? I'm not sure, but it's something I'm constantly thinking about and have yet come up with a completely sufficient answer.

Michael: Sure, I'm happy with that friendly amendment. We're better served having our egos kneecapped and hobbled and nursed back to a humbler health, rather than executed. Everything belongs in its proper place. Names are certainly useful when we talk to one another, and, like you, I'm not sure that would be possible without having the concept of an ego. It's a confusing subject, to be sure.

Matthew: It is confusing! But maybe that's okay. Maybe it doesn't really matter. Maybe what matters is living in the present moment regardless of our concepts. I'm sure we have shit to learn in this life, but perhaps the biggest thing we can learn is how to live in the moment regardless of our understanding of concepts.

Michael: It seems to me that a person who is conceptually off-base but always living in the present is further along the spiritual path than the egghead space cadet.

Matthew: Probably. I will say, however, that if we are too "out there" with our concepts—that is, if our concepts are so off-base that they fail to have any meaning whatsoever—it's going to be difficult to live in the present. For instance, if we believe "hell" means being eternally tortured apart from God and we always live in the moment with that in the back of our minds, then we're probably going to have a difficult time actually living in the moment. At least, that was the case for me. When I held to eternal conscious torment as an eschatological certainty, the present moment was all but impossible to enjoy because I was so damn afraid of what could happen in the future. I know not everyone has this experience, but it was all too true for me.

Michael: Another friendly amendment taken. On some issues, with respect to the present moment, it's very important what we believe, such as eschatology, or climate change (if we believe climate change isn't human-driven, then our future present moments will be shitty and all our fault). I guess what I was trying to say is that the point of life will never be an object of knowledge. It is about the actual location, not the map that got you there.

Matthew: Ain't that the truth! But oh, how we love to confuse the map for the territory, the menu for the meal. I think it makes us feel all warm and cozy inside, thinking that if we could only gather the correct knowledge about something, or have the correct God-inspired book in our hands, then we'd be solid. But more often than not, we only miss the moment when we focus too heavily on these endeavors. They are important, sure, but in reality, they are secondary issues. First and foremost is the present moment. And speaking of which, I think it's time to stoke this fire and refill our glasses. What say you?

Michael: I'll drink to that. Cheers!

·· 6 ··
MIDNIGHT

Matthew: Now that we got the fire blazing and the booze flowing, I guess my question is this: How do we get people to realize that all we really have is the moment before us? How do we get people to accept the fact that enlightenment, the kingdom of God—whatever you wanna call it—is always presently right in front of our noses? Is it as simple as meditation? As focusing on breathing in and breathing out? Or is there much more to this whole contemplative living?

Michael: Well, eventually the present moment is gonna have to stand on its own two legs and justify itself. Meditation is a good way of doing that. You don't know what the non-conceptualized present is all about until you actually experience it.

Matthew: True. We don't know what anything is all about until we actually experience it. That's the thing about experience: it's a type of knowing that is unknowable until we actually taste it. I just wonder what it is about those who experience the beautifully naked present moment. Why do some have that sticky-icky while some are left with nothing but Snicklefritz (if you catch my meaning)? Is it simply a case of the latter not wanting to get out of their heads? Are they too scared to let go of their need for doctrinal certainty? Maybe both/and, as well as a whole bunch of other reasons?

Michael: I'm inclined to say that those left underwhelmed haven't really experienced the naked now. To these people, the sights, sounds, smells, feelings, and tastes of this world are being diluted by something else—some concept. I think it's important to point out that the present moment won't always bring about ecstasy. But there should always be an abiding sense of peace, which should never fail to impress. Of course, I say this tentatively.

Matthew: If I'm being completely honest, everything we say about spiritual matters should be done tentatively. I only know what it's like to be me and you only know what it's like to be you. And sure, we can share what our subjective experiences are like around a bonfire, but at the end of the day, we all see and taste things a tad differently. In other words, while we are all the same in a way—human—we all process life's experiences in different ways and come at things from different angles. So, what works for one person may not entirely work for another. And while we can put forth ideas that may help others rest in the power of Present, these ideas and guides are, well, tentative. But one thing that *does* seem universal is that any concept that hinders the naked now needs to be held more loosely. White knuckled clinching never seems like a good idea. That, I say much less tentatively.

Michael: Everyone's story is different, that's for sure. If there was only a single narrative, you'd have to think we'd have the method for salvation down to a science. But alas, such is not the case. Realizing this can be scary and sobering at times—knowing that it's ultimately up to you. But it also means that nobody gets to judge how you choose to go about life. It's a trade-off that I'm willing to make.

Matthew: And yet, judging is still right in the human wheel-house. In fact, it seems like the go-to Evangelical approach to "saving souls," does it not? In their minds, they've got the secret formula for salvation and how we should all go about living our lives. Their authority? A quasi-scientific—and might I say, starkly rigid—approach to an ancient text called "The Bible." In other words, they look outside themselves and the spirit that dwells within for ultimate authority, never realizing what you and I have long since discovered, namely that it's up to each and every one of us to look inside in order to figure out how best to traverse the path to enlightenment. Is it any wonder, then, why Christianity in America is such a shitshow?

Michael: Shitshow is a strong term, but I'll take it. I would also add "ineffective." Twenty-five years of following this Jesus Evangelicals claim to love so much simply didn't work for me. It did nothing to help me feel at peace. Forcing myself to sit down for ten minutes a day and focus on my breath, however, actually does something. I think it works on two levels. There's the act itself—of getting your mind off whatever is bothering you—and then there's the knowledge that you're the one that's in control, rather than some outside source.

Matthew: Being in control really scares a lot of people, though. Religious people, especially, seem keen on giving up their author-ity to an outside source. Call it Jesus. Call it the Bible. Call it whatever. But there always seems to be some outside authority

83

that they'd rather defer to. Maybe it's because they see themselves—and everyone, really—as nothing but depraved piles of shit. They may not put it in such terms, but when you listen to certain Christians, it's as if self-deprecation is the highest form of flattery found in the known universe.

You said something, though, that I think would help take people a long way toward realizing how powerful the present moment can be, which is that each and every one of us is in control of things. If you want to put it in Christian terms, each and every one of us has the Christ in us. If you want to use Buddhist terms, we are all Atman. Regardless, I think the point is that authority is found within.

Michael: Along with seeing themselves as piles of shit, maybe people are afraid of the responsibility of being in control. While it's true that nobody gets to judge how you choose to live your life, there's also nobody but yourself to blame (in most cases) if it's not shaping up the way you'd like. This applies not only to the circumstances that you find yourself in (again, in most cases), but also how you choose to react to those circumstances. There's always something to be grateful for in life, but some people—myself included—choose to be addicted to shitty moods.

Matthew: I'll agree with you to a certain extent. That is, for many, only *they* are to blame for having a shitty life, or a shitty perspective on life. It seems that a lot of people, however, are in circumstances that are well beyond their control. People born in countries that are war-torn, for instance. Or those born into abusive situations where they've been traumatized since the day they showed up on the scene. For these folks, it's much more complicated. At the end of the day, though, I think you're correct: we can choose how to react to our circumstances. And no amount of wallowing in self-pity is actually going to help things. It sucks, but sometimes you really do have to pick yourself up by the bootstraps, not because that's how things should be, but simply because life can be a bitch and no one else is gonna do it for you.

Michael: I appreciate you pushing back. I don't deny there's such a thing as being a victim of circumstances, and I find the people that do deny it really annoying. And stupid. But I also don't want to deny the power of human volition. Even if there's no reasonable chance of much "upward movement"—in whatever sphere you wanna talk about—I think there's always room to make your circumstances better, even if it's just an improved attitude, which is huge. I mean, if you were never anything but grateful about your situation in life, what more could you ask for? But again, as you just touched on, some people are in really shitty circumstances, and perhaps putting the pressure of trying to be happy on top of it would be the proverbial straw.

Matthew: That's absolutely right. Trying to be happy in shitty circumstances really does seem like an exercise in futility. Plus, being happy and being grateful are quite different concepts. For instance, one can be totally grateful for what they have in life and still not be "happy" with things like economic injustices, racist family members, violence against children, and so on. Or, speaking more personally, because I suffer from depression, I don't find myself in a "happy" mood all that often, but am still grateful for my life: my family, friends, talents, etc.

But now to the point about human volition. Isn't it interesting that, on the one hand, we do in fact have a free will of sorts, but also that it is quite impacted by predetermined circumstances that are well out of our control? It sounds paradoxical, and maybe it is, but it seems true nonetheless. Perhaps that's why the greatest philosophers of our day—Tom Talbott, David Bentley Hart, and even your father, Ric—all talk about true, human freedom as that which always chooses the good. It's not so much about making choices that are seemingly free; it's about viewing things for what they truly are, having the mental, ethical, and spiritual eyes to see what is good and true and right, and then acting accordingly. And when we have these things in order, the choice becomes so clear that there really wasn't a choice at all.

Michael: I only care that my choices *appear* to be free. Even if my life is completely scripted, as long as I *feel* like my choices are independent—that certain things in this world couldn't happen unless I made a "choice" to act—that's all I care about. And, as Eric Reitan would put it, libertarian free will doesn't even seem worth having. I don't want the ability to make choices that would fuck up my life. I want the ability to see life clearly and act accordingly. If that means I don't have free will, then so be it. I don't really care.

Matthew: It is quite absurd how some folks tend to think about human volition. As if the highest form of what it means to be free is in the ability to make the shittiest decisions ever. They'll say, "Well, people choose to go to hell. What could God have done about it?" Oh, I don't know, made a better kind of free will. I mean, how can we call someone free when they're willing to shove their face into a fire and hold it there for all of eternity? Sort of raises the question, *what do you mean by free,* doesn't it? To that end, I'm with you and Reitan; that sort of freedom is obviously not worth having.

Michael: As usual, it probably has something to do with pride, with the ego. If I'm able to choose God and reject the devil it must be because there's something special about me. But if choice has nothing to do with my worthiness then that means I don't get to look down my nose at anyone. Screw that!

Matthew: That's something that always confuses me to no end. If someone uses their free will to make the right choice about God, then didn't they obviously have a better will than those who reject God? To ask it another way, what makes the free will of those who choose God over the devil so much better than those who choose the opposite? To my mind, then, something other than a purely libertarian, autonomous will is at play here.

Michael: Do people choose to have shitty wills? No, obviously. If I had my druthers, I would choose a will that always wants what is for the best, and I would choose to be a white American male, obviously.

Matthew: Haha! But haven't you learned anything from Ben Shapiro? White privilege is a myth. Wink, wink. But seriously, the only shitty will is an enslaved will. And all free wills are not necessarily free to choose right or wrong, but free to always choose rightly. What does that look like in practical terms? That's the million-dollar question. It's about choosing whatever is good, true, loving, gracious, beautiful, and so on. You know, what Aquinas might call the transcendentals.

Michael: Well, I think that if you look at your life and can honestly say that it's flourishing, you probably don't have an enslaved will. Like I said earlier, I don't think God is into playing mind games. I think he wants the answer to that question to be pretty obvious.

Matthew: Definitely! A caveat, however: it depends on what you mean by flourishing. I'm sure you mean "spiritually flourishing," because a lot of enslaved folks are financially flourishing, but many of them seem to be spiritually dead. Take Trump for instance. That dude has all the money in the world and seems to be a hollow shell of a spiritual person. He's got consumerist Christianity down to a T, but in terms of enlightenment—and I can only speculate because I don't know the man (nor do I necessarily want to)—he seems as enslaved as anyone. Enslaved to the desire for power. Enslaved to a narcissistic mind. All that. You know, it's as if the Ring of Power is around his neck.

Michael: Yes, thank you, I meant spiritual flourishing. Peace is a sign of spiritual flourishing—"fruit of the spirit," if you will— and I don't necessarily see that in Trump. I see an empty husk flailing about, a superego not able to let go. I also fail to see much love or joy or patience or kindness or goodness or faithfulness or self-control. Not that I'm judging.

Matthew: I don't take that as judging. It's more about observing. Plus, we all make judgments in life and that isn't necessarily a bad thing. Judgmentalism is, sure. But not judging as such. There is a huge difference. We have to make judgments: do I eat this thing that is poisonous? No, I judge that to be a shitty decision. So, the problem isn't making judgments. It's judging others to a standard one fails to judge themselves with. That's the key issue. And when one is spiritually flourishing, they need not point the accusatory finger at others. They realize it's best to focus on one's own journey because, at the end of the day, all we can really control is ourselves.

Michael: Which is just as well, really. Forget being spiritually woke, normally I simply don't have the energy to be judgmental. All my energy is typically spent on selfish endeavors. But Donald Trump has the potential to truly complicate my life, along with the rest of America, and I don't think I can handle anything more than my rich, White People problems, so I feel like I have to speak up.

Matthew: Wow, thank you for your honesty. To be frank, even the most "selfless" among us probably are quite selfish. It's not a bad thing, it just means that, for the most part, most of us probably only think of our own personal issues, and not the issues of others. That's just how life seems to work. Sure, we all like to think of ourselves as selfless saints, but in reality, we are all probably quite selfish. Meaning, when it comes down to it, the majority of our energy is spent on our own personal circum-stances. I know that is the reality of my situation. I like to think of myself as someone who focuses my energy on what others are going through, but when it comes down to it, I probably fixate on what I personally have to deal with on the day to day. It's not something I'm proud of, but it's the reality of the situation.

Which, again, brings me back to the adage: judge not lest ye be judged. I can't really be a judgmental asshole because life is such that I need to sweep off my own porch, first and foremost.

Michael: You hit on something with "that's just how life seems to work." Humans can only experience life from a single perspective, from a "self." So, even if you're being completely "selfless," by giving to the poor or whatever, that experience for you is technically selfish. I reckon that experience is quite fulfilling, but it's selfish. So, life just seems to work in a way where being selfish and being selfless can be one and the same thing.

Matthew: Funny, that. It's important to remember, however—lest we find ourselves lining up with Ayn Rand here—that our focus shouldn't be on selfish things. Sure, as the old adage goes, it's better to give than to receive, and that by giving we, the giver, feel good about what we are doing, but our focus, first and foremost, shouldn't be on how such an act makes us feel. That's secondary. We do good for the other for the sake of goodness itself, not because it makes our ego feel all tingly inside. At least, I think that's how it's supposed to work. I don't know; it's getting late, the fire is dying down, and my drink is empty… so, you know, the old brain is getting kinda foggy.

Michael: Mine, too. Let's call it a night and just assume we solved all the world's problems in one sitting.

Matthew: That's always a safe assumption, my friend. 'Night.

Michael: 'Night.

Autumn

TWILIGHT

Matthew: Well, here we are again, sitting down for yet another Session. I hope you put enough fuel on this bad-boy because it's chilly as fuck.

Michael: Of course. But just in case, here's some more "warm stuff" for your glass.

Matthew: Appreciated. And cheers, mate!

Michael: Cheers, my friend!

Matthew: You know, if I've gotta be honest, the timing of this session couldn't be more appropriate. Autumn is my favorite season, sure—what with all the glorious yellows, reds, and oranges—but it's still an odd time of year. Because, if you *really* think about it, it's a season of death and decay, and as I write this, I'm watching my grandfather die right before my eyes. While this saddens me beyond words, I can't help but think that for him, in some weird way, it's also a bit of a beautiful thing. Before anyone accuses me of being overwhelmingly macabre, it needs to be known that my grandmother died ten years ago—on Halloween, 2009, to be exact—and while I can't confirm that when my grandfather passes away, he will reunite with her, it *seems* to be true. That is, it seems like the best ending to their story. And, you know, I find beauty in that. But I don't know, man; I'm literally just sharing what's running through my head at the moment, so forgive me if that's not the best jumping-off point for this conversation.

Michael: Best jumping-off point? We're just having a chat. It's not like we're writing a book or anything.

So, sorry about your grandfather, bro. But, like you, I have this feeling, this "knowing" even, that he will be reunited with his bride. If all the leaves on the trees fell down, never to come back, that would straightforwardly suck ass. But we're just saying goodbye for a little while, which no doubt sucks, but I think we'll cherish our loved ones—as with the leaves—all the more when we do see them again.

Matthew: Dude, I hope so. This life can be a bitch, but I can't help but think it's only a bitch for a season. I'm not trying to be a complete fatalist, you know? Fatalistic some of the time, of course, but not one through and through.

Michael: It had better only be for a season. I can't take much more of this shit—and I'm one of the lucky ones! All things considered; my life is pretty damn good. But, the sense of loss— after the fire—is starting to get to me. Paradise is starting to bounce back: lots are cleared up, houses are being built, et cetera, et cetera. But I miss all the trees. I didn't think I'd be saying that, because Paradise had way too many trees, but I'm realizing that they were part of what made Paradise, Paradise. They made it home. And it will never be like that again.

Matthew: Not so fast, homie. I just read that they recently planted over 700 trees all over town, so give it some time. And remember the lesson learned by the Hobbits at the end of *The Return of the King*. After they lost the party tree that grew south of Bag End in Hobbiton, they were miserable and forlorn. That is, until Samwise Gamgee planted an enchanted Mallorn tree in its place. And while it could never replace the old tree where Bilbo gave his farewell speech, it helped in healing those who were saddened by the deep sense of loss. So, think of Paradise as the Shire and your property—with our abundant garden and orchard—as Bag End. Sure, it has been razed, but such destruction only lasts for a period, and one day soon it will come back even stronger and more imbued with beauty.

Michael: Fair enough. Don't think I fail in appreciating a hopeful future. But I still think it's appropriate to mourn what has been lost, even if it's followed by a superior future. I'll miss our gigantic piss-tree. It's seemingly gone forever, and that's sad. I'll miss our old house, even if our new one will be bigger and better. I don't see how it's possible, but I hope they both—the piss-tree and the old house—have a solid belonging in the future.

Matthew: I totally get that, and agree with you. Loss should be grieved. Pain should be felt. To simply "move on" from loss is to not feel life. And just because you can hope for a beautiful future doesn't mean that sorrow experienced in the past loses its weight or gravity. Perhaps what is needed is balance. Grieve what is lost. Feel the pain deeply. Shed some tears. There is a time for all that, just like there is a time to hope, a time to plan the rebuilding process, and then a time to actually get your hands dirty and put it all together. As long as through it all you don't wobble, right?

Michael: I suppose that's the biggest take away: don't wobble. Whatever you do in life, commit to it. Here I am talking about mourning the past, but some people aren't sentimental like that. Maybe they're technically dead inside, but that's okay. It's okay to be dead inside. Or, maybe their past isn't worth mourning; there's no point in mustering feelings that are fake.

Matthew: Is it okay to be dead inside, though? I mean, okay in one way, sure; I wouldn't want to pile guilt on someone who fails to feel alive. But at the same time, are those who are dead inside okay with it? Probably not. They just don't know how to turn the light on. Speaking from experience, whenever I have suffered through the worst that my depression has to offer me, failing to get through it quickly has never been for lack of trying. I've wanted to be free from feeling dead inside, but sometimes there is just no other option except, to wait it out until the storm passes. And for some, that storm doesn't seem to pass, or if it does, passes at a snail's pace.

Michael: Well, I think it's okay to be dead inside for a season. I mean, it's not a life-threatening condition, so in that sense it's okay. Our ultimate goal is everlasting joy and abundant life, I believe, and maybe part of getting to that point is going through depression. And, trying to rush the process, as you pointed out, is futile, so we might as well get as comfortable with it as possible. Things bloom in their own time.

Matthew: Again, it's all a balancing act. Life can suck. Depression sucks. And there seems to be no way out of the situation. There is only going through it and hoping that in the end, all will be well. That's one reason why I'm a Universalist. I just don't see any other endgame that makes sense. I mean, if *all* is not well in the end—and when I say *all*, I mean *all*—then we might as well become nihilists. And I don't want to embrace that philosophy so I guess I'm just left with a more hopeful ending. I'll take it though, because it at least makes me feel better than the hopeless alternative most Christians seem to embrace.

Michael: The biggest reason why I'm a Universalist is because it makes me feel better—not necessarily about the fate of others, but about my own. If I'm brutally honest, I really only care that I make it to heaven. And if everyone is assured that they'll make it, that means that my spot is assured. But who am I, if not a specific point of view in the universe, one defined by its surroundings? In other words, if my surroundings don't make it to heaven, then neither do I.

Matthew: Well, aside from the fact that you don't care if I make it to heaven or not, I think I actually agree with the main *thrust* of your point. That is, we are so interconnected that what happens to one happens to all. If you don't make it into God's afterparty in the sky, for example, then heaven's gonna suck for me. And if that's the case, can we really call it heaven? It certainly wouldn't be as good a time as if you had made it in. The conversations wouldn't be nearly as beneficial. The hikes up Sawmill Peak would be rather boring. And I'd have no one to stoke the firepit. So, all in all, I think heaven at that point would be hell.

Michael: Don't worry, I'll make it to heaven. It's you that I'm worried about; you are *super* racist, my friend, and I don't think God is down with that. And that's a shame, because you bring out a part of me that nobody else does, and I like it (and I'm not talking about the racism). A part of me literally won't make it to heaven once you're inevitably condemned.

Matthew: Oh, fuck right off! I'm not one of those racist MAGA twats. Not that all Trump supporters are racist fuck-holes, but… maybe a little? Don't be so arrogant though; if only one of us is getting in, it's definitely me. I'm way more Jesus-y than you, while being much more humble than you would understand (to quote the Stable Orange Genius). So, I think it will be me who suffers in heaven because of your hellbound soul.

Michael: You *are* way more Jesus-y than me, that's for sure, and in certain circles that would make up for your over-the-top racism. I guess only time will tell which of us is worthy. Winner gets to escape the flames!

Matthew: I know you are joking about my supposed racism, but let's talk about that. Let's get serious for just a moment. Are people with lighter skin automatically racist because they benefit from structures that oppress those with more melanin? Some would say so. I'm not sure, though. It's still something I'm working through. I mean, I won't deny that having lighter skin affords folks benefits that Blacks, for example, don't have—like not worrying about being shot for having weed on your person. However, at the same time, if you are against those exact structures that oppress folks, and actively speak out against them, does that still make you racist? I struggle with such a suggestion. Plus, not that long ago, my people—Sicilian immigrants—were oppressed because of their darker skin. Some even got lynched by white folks in the South, and suffered under Jim Crow laws. So, that's why I struggle with the term "racist." I feel like it gets flung around too flippantly sometimes. To my mind, the majority of the conversation needs to move from the personal to the systemic, from calling individuals racist to calling cultural, societal, and political structures racist in their orientation. Thoughts?

Michael: I totally agree. I thought that racism was the belief that one's own race is superior and has the right to dominate others. There is, however, such a thing as laziness, and I don't think we should conflate the two. Let's take police harassment as an example. I, as a white person, tend to get noticed less by the police than a Black person does. I'm less likely to be a victim of random traffic stops, and if I happen to have weed on me, probably won't get thrown in jail. I don't think it automatically makes *me* racist if this happens. It might mean that I'm lazy if I don't also fight for equality. But I myself am not actively dominating a Black person, and I don't think that Black people—all things being equal—are more likely to be criminals. The police officer, however, might be racist.

Matthew: That's a fair point. Like I said before, I don't think it's *that* important to talk about individual racism; it's certainly not as important as talking about systemic racial injustices. Sure, it's important for the individual to befriend those of other races, colors, creeds, and sexual orientations, because that's how things can change on the micro-level, but for things to change on the macro-level, we need to dismantle the structures that keep the racist status quo in place. And, to be totally frank, white folks need to take a backseat in this conversation and let folks of color do most of the talking. Not because what white folks have to say isn't important at all, but simply because most of the talking about this issue has been done by white dudes, so now is as good a time as any to do some listening.

Michael: I think there needs to be a dialogue, for sure, but white people should predominantly be introspective and listen. For example, I've heard it thrown around that because there's not much visible racism here in Paradise, California, that must mean that racism doesn't exist anywhere in the United States. Well, Paradise is a small—very small, now—mostly white community, so it's not exactly a good representation of America. We white folk need to trust that when Black people give reports of their encounters with the law, or other situations where racism is overtly evident, that they're telling the truth. How we get Whitey to do that, I don't know.

Matthew: Two words: Contact Hypothesis. Racist white folks need properly managed contact with Black and brown folks, which should in theory reduce stereotyping, prejudice, and discrimination. Now, this obviously isn't the end-all-be-all solution to the problem, but actually getting to know those against whom you are prejudiced helps. How we turn the entire ship in the right direction, I'm not sure. It's a big fucking ship, and these things take a long time to course-correct. And while we aren't there yet, it seems progress is being made. Sometimes it's one step forward and two steps back, but overall, I'm sure it's better than it was 100 years ago.

Michael: Things are getting better. I can't remember the last time a Black man got lynched. I take that back; the police do it all the time. But it's not as often as it was in the early 1900s. It's generally considered offensive for a non-Black to say the "n-word"—and other things. Human beings are wired to notice and remember negative phenomena more than positive phenomena, so it's important to step back every once in a while, to reflect on the actual situation. Everything's gonna be fine—I say that being slightly tipsy, mind you.

Matthew: To be fair, most of us are slightly tipsy these days. We're writing this as the coronavirus is fucking shit up, so, fuck it, what else is there to do?

Michael: I hear people are copulating, creating the so-called "Coronial" generation. That sounds nice. I'm also down for gaming.

Matthew: I'm down for fornicating and gaming, but not making any more babies. One is enough for me. Plus, it seems like we've got too many people in this world as it is, and I'm not trying to exacerbate humanity's issues right now. Either that, or we're just too damn greedy and because of that, Mother Earth ain't all too pleased. Global Warming. Viral Pandemics. Deforestation. The depopulation of the bees. A bunch of other scary shit. One way or another, it seems like something's coming to a head, so sexual protection of some kind is what I'm recommending these days.

Michael: Things certainly feel apocalyptic, but I think it's because we're not all living like hippies—or Native Americans. I'm pretty sure climate change wouldn't be an issue if industrialization never happened.

Matthew: Right. For all that the industrialized world has given us—dope-ass cars, motorcycles you can nearly kill yourself with, Wi-Fi, video games, Chuck Taylors, sex toys—it certainly has messed things up. Royally. And you're right: We are at an apocalyptic point in human history. And by that I don't mean it's literally the end of the world, and that all the good Christians will be raptured to heaven. I just mean apocalyptic in the most literal sense of the Greek word. That is to say, it's a time of unveiling and revealing. We are coming to the place where we are going to have to make some big decisions as a species. Climate change can't continue to spiral out of control. The bee populations need to be restored. The coral reefs can't continue to be killed off at unprecedented rates. Because, if all these things continue to happen, we are fucked. The Earth will live on. She'll just do it without most, if not all, of us. So, it's time to change course—and quickly!

Michael: I'm pessimistic about the whole situation, unfortunately. I'm scared. There's a good chance we're too late in reversing climate change. Donald Trump will get re-elected. COVID-19 will kill a third of Earth's population. One day I'll become impotent. I've always wanted to live like a hermit though, so at least I'll have some peace and quiet until the planet is destroyed.

With that, I've gotta take a piss. Be right back.

··· 8 ···
DUSK

Michael: Okay, I'm back.

Matthew: Need a topping off?

Michael: In these times? Always.

Matthew: Cheers!

Michael: Cheers!

Matthew: Let me go back to something you said earlier; while I share some of your pessimism, I think I'm a little more optimistic. Trump may be reelected, sure. There may not be anything we can do about that. But I think we can do something about climate change. I mean, it's a giant ship, so turning this motherfucker is gonna take a while, but I hold out hope that we'll do it. And COVID-19 won't kill a third of us. Maybe a third will get infected when it's all said and done, but most will recover. I don't know, perhaps my subtle optimism is unwarranted, but I still feel that if we fight for environmental justice and for the common good of both our species and the planet, we can stem the tide.

Michael: I suppose my point would be that I'm no longer surprised by anything. Can we rally against climate change? Maybe. Chances are equally good that we won't. Survival is never guaranteed. Knowing that's the case is a good thing, of course. It gets us off our asses.

Matthew: Ain't that the truth! It seems that our psychology is such that we need to be jolted once in a while—just like when Frodo had to flee the Shire. He always *wanted* to have an adventure similar to his uncle Bilbo, but never took the chance until it was forced upon him. We, too, are at such a moment, and we have two choices: 1) to sit idly by in the Shire and pretend the world isn't burning around us or, 2) save the Shire by heading out, perhaps even to Mordor, if need be. But there is a caveat: Frodo isn't the only hero of the story. In fact, perhaps he's not even *the* hero of the story. In other words, we can all do our part, large or small. So, whether we are Sam, Merry, Pippen, or any of the other characters, we only bring down the Tower—i.e. heal the planet—by working together and doing our part.

Michael: I'd say it's all about what you want to accomplish, and I wouldn't even necessarily put it in moral terms. It's about coming to terms with what you really want to get out of this life. It's like that scene from *The Notebook*: "What do you want?!" It's time to make a decision. Do you want to live in a world that isn't fucking on fire? Well, that means you're gonna have to do certain things to limit carbon emissions. I'm sorry, but those are the rules. Do you not give a shit? Well, soldier on, I guess.

Matthew: And that's what concerns me—there are a whole lot of people who don't give a shit. So many of us are just a bunch of orcs doing Saruman's bidding: tree after tree, felled to the ground. But hey, we must remember Gandalf's sage advice: "It is not our part to master all the tides of the world, but to do what is in us for the succour of those years wherein we are set, uprooting the evil in the fields that we know, so that those who live after may have clean earth to till. What weather they shall have is not ours to rule."[1] In other words, if we want to do our part—as you and I do—then we should simply do our part. What others do and what comes their way is not up to us. So, the question is: What do we want to do?

Michael: I want to live on a healthy planet Earth. The problem with democracy is that everyone gets a say, even the dumb-dumbs. We need a philosopher king, a wise ruler who can grab the country—or, dare I say, the planet?—by the scruff of its neck and make it do the right thing.

Matthew: The problem with that, however, is that those who typically rise to the top let the power go to their head. May I again refer to Tolkien for some wisdom? When Galadriel has the One Ring right in front of her, she sees what it will cause her to become. Gandalf, too, must reject the urge to do something about the Ring. Both would have had good intentions in wielding it, but both would have succumbed to the temptations it would have inevitably brought. So, too, the philosopher king.

....

1 Tolkien, J.R.R. *The Return of the King*. New York: Houghton Mifflin, 1955, 861.

Maybe what we need is a Hobbit; a tiller of the Earth and a smoker of pipe-weed.

Michael: A Hobbit with absolute power?

Matthew: Well, put better yet—and maybe I'm contradicting myself now—a Hobbit who is able to resist such power. The sobering truth about this—which is something that Tolkien absolutely nails—is that even the Good Hobbit doesn't resist it in the end. As I've said on numerous occasions around the crackling fire, without Smeagol, the Ring never gets thrown into the chasm. In other words, even a noble Hobbit falls prey to the power the Ring falsely promises. So, I guess that is the long way of saying that I have no fucking clue how to run things. All I know is I would make a terrible philosopher king. And I would be better suited to gardening in the Shire than venturing out to Mordor. But maybe that's just the philosophy one needs in order to prove they are up for the journey.

Michael: You can only put so much faith in human vessels, for sure. But when I recommend a philosopher king, I assume that he will be a great philosopher—loving knowledge and wisdom and acting accordingly. As king (or queen) they will also be a great leader. Hobbits may be wise, but I wouldn't consider them leaders like Aragorn. I think we need to dismiss the idea, especially in the age of Trump, that there's no such thing as a good politician.

Matthew: Totally. And like you've said to me before, just because we can't have the best option doesn't mean we shouldn't go for the next best thing. Put into practice: just because we can't have the philosopher king doesn't mean we should say "fuck it all" and allow someone like Trump to get four more years. I know it's tempting, but it's kind of dangerous given how shitty a leader he is.

Michael: If I could say a little more on the matter, there's obviously a reason why I said *philosopher* king, and not something like *engineer* king. Any kind of expertise is never going to be a bad thing, but if the engineer king is generally knowledgeable and wise, it wasn't his understanding of structural code that made him so. Even a born leader needs to know where the country should go, and that is a question of philosophy, not leadership.

Matthew: So, are you saying that Trump isn't the philosopher king? I mean, he *does* have a philosophy, albeit a fairly incomprehensible and contradictory one.

Michael: By all accounts, he doesn't enjoy reading, which isn't a good sign.

Matthew: No, it never is. I think it was Mark Twain who said something like, "A person who doesn't read has no advantage over a person who can't."[2] And whether Trump reads or not, I doubt many of his supporters do (unless they're reading QAnon bullshit). That's probably why so many of them deny climate

---

2 This is likely not an actual quote by Twain, as it cannot be verified by any of his writings, though it is often attested to him.

science, or any science for that matter. I know that's quite a broad-brush statement, but hey, this is a conversation, not a dissertation.

Michael: It's probably a more accurate statement than anyone should feel comfortable with. I don't understand this business of being skeptical of expertise and education. It's like, if you don't trust scientists to talk straight about climate change, then who are you gonna trust? Conservative pastors? What, exactly, do these people think it means to be educated?

Matthew: Honestly, I have no clue. I don't think many conservative pastors value education. It seems many of the more fundamentalist persuasion think that all institutions of higher education are part of some liberal agenda that is hellbent on crushing Christianity. Or, as they might put it, that scientific experts are a part of "the world," so often besmirched from the pulpit. I've tried to talk to these folks about climate change and I've yet to get anywhere. It's strange. I guess some people are just fine with watching the world burn, and don't believe there is anything to this notion of cause and effect. That is to say, to their mind human beings couldn't *possibly* have anything to do with destroying the planet. Consider me baffled by this, because to *my* mind, it's pretty fucking obvious that we do.

Michael: One response I've heard is that it's arrogant to think that humans have the power to damage the planet and change the environment; I guess because it's somehow overriding the sovereignty of God. But, arrogant? How is it arrogant to think that humans can abuse power? Power doesn't impress me any longer. Power is for the fourth-grade Christian. You want to impress me? Show some fucking foresight and restraint.

Matthew: And, take climate change out of the conversation for a moment, because I know that can be politicized. Isn't it fantastically obvious that we damage and change the environment? I mean, do people not pay attention to the world around them? Are they not aware that there is a garbage patch twice the size of Texas in the Pacific Ocean? Do they not care that the coral reefs are dying? That ocean life is choking to death on plastics? That the Amazon is vanishing due to us bulldozing it down for our Olympic stadiums? That the Chinese government has to broadcast sunrises and sunsets on TV due to their pollution levels? So ...arrogant? Yes, but only if we think that we would *not* have a damaging effect on the planet.

Michael: To be fair, I get the impression that most people are aware of and care about the sorry state of affairs. However, I also think that percentage takes a nosedive in the United States.

Matthew: Sadly, I think you're right. I've noticed just how little we care about litter, for instance, these past few months as I've walked our highways, picking up trash. Compare our roads with those in Ireland, where I visited last year, and there is a striking difference. It's as if they actually care about their land, while we only wax poetic about how great we are. That shit breaks my heart, to be honest, because instead of living in the Shire, I feel like I'm trapped in Isengard while Orcs destroy the precious trees around me.

Michael: If you take into account one of the predominant worldviews in the United States, the situation makes sense—or, it at least makes some sort of sense to me. Evangelical Christians believe that this world is not our own; heaven is where we should be storing our treasures. So, it doesn't really matter, in an ultimate sense, if we pollute, or if the climate changes. I hope that we'll snap out of it and take care of our heavenly planet a little better, but I'm not sure we'll know how.

Matthew: Can I share something with you?

Michael: Shoot.

Matthew: The Bible these folks love so much—one could say worship, even—says that heaven is here and now, that it is in our midst. Remember that prayer Jesus tells us to pray? *Thy kingdom come, thy will be done, on earth as it is in heaven*. I do. Apparently, they don't. Because no matter what we think about the afterlife, no matter what we think heaven is like, our goal is to bring heaven to earth. You'd think Christians, then, would be the ones leading the charge in changing the planet for the better.

Michael: You'd think so. However, first of all, these people are also American, and Americans have fetishized their way of life, which unfortunately, includes not giving a shit about how it impacts the rest of the planet. Second: we're lazy, and change is difficult.

Matthew: It's really odd to me that for Americans, caring about the climate has become a political issue. Liberals seem to want to curb climate change while Conservatives think it's a hoax. That makes no sense to me. It just goes to show you that we can find a way to politically divide from one another, even if that which we divide over isn't political at all. In my wildest imagination, I couldn't imagine ever dividing over whether to care for the planet or not.

Michael: Should I say it? I'm gonna say it. The two political parties are not morally equivalent. Democrats are humans and therefore imperfect, but let's be clear-eyed about how morally bankrupt the Republicans have become, especially after selling their soul to Trump. Protecting the planet should not be a pet project of the Democrats. Protecting the immigrants should not be a pet project of the Democrats, either. I could go on.

Matthew: Right? It's almost as if we've forgotten the poem emblazoned on the Statue of Liberty: "Give me your tired, your poor, your huddled masses yearning to breathe free . . ."[3] Either that, or we've decided we don't give a shit. Trump's made that clear, and so have his sycophants. They want nothing to do with those coming from so-called "shithole countries." His words, not mine. My, how we've lost our ever-lovin' way!

Michael: I don't think it's necessarily that Americans stopped caring; I think it's that we've become afraid. We'd like to help the immigrants, but we're too afraid that they'll steal our strawberry-picking jobs, and rape our women, and we hate them for that. But, to paraphrase the immortal words of Jim Jeffries: hate

---

3 From Emma Lazarus' 1883 sonnet entitled "The New Colossus."

cannot defeat hate, only love can. And wouldn't you know it: perfect love casts out fear.

Matthew: Yeah, but we've got these so-called leaders, stoking the flames of fear among the masses of typically white, conservative Evangelicals. It's not just them, though. We all default to fearing the "other," whether they be a different color, creed, or sexual orientation. It just gets exacerbated by certain leaders, who use fear to pander to a certain voter base. And I know you know of whom I speak.

Michael: It's Trump. You're talking about Trump, right?

Matthew: Obvi! But it's not just him. He's the symptom of a much greater disease. Think about it. Someone like Trump could never have been elected in a healthy society. This shit runs much deeper.

Michael: More fundamentally, I would say that Donald J. Trump as we know him today wouldn't even exist if society were healthy. A healthy society doesn't allow for xenophobia, narcissism, racism, cronyism, or orange skin.

Matthew: I'm sure there would still be anomalies, but overall, you're right. We're all responsible for this mess. It reminds me of a passage from the book of Genesis, when, after Abel gets murdered, God asks Cain what happened and where his brother went. Cain retorts, "Am I my brother's keeper?" And the implied answer is, "Yes!!!" It goes back to this whole notion of human volition. We are, of course, responsible for our own actions, whether we've been dealt a great hand, or we got the short end of the stick. But, that doesn't mean we aren't also responsible for one another. And to be perfectly honest, we have no one to blame but ourselves for this clusterfuck we are in.

Michael: I mean, who or what else could we blame? The parts are the system, and the system is the parts. But I don't like the language of blame, anyhow. It isn't helpful. Everyone bears essentially equal amounts of blame, so there's really no cause for the shame it ultimately causes.

Matthew: Ah, good ole shame! A favorite tool in the belt of the religious—like its first cousin, fear. Both are used incredibly well in keeping us from making progress as a species. When used in combination, they paralyze. Sadly, that's the place where too many of us live. Maybe that's one reason we don't up and change the systems we live under. We're trapped, and would rather hide under our covers, than get out there and do some reforming.

Michael: Shame on those in power! They know exactly what they're doing, those cheeky bastards. They know how to keep people in line. I'll bet such positions of power give the stiffest woodies. But honestly, I can't blame them. If I had access to such pleasures, I'm pretty sure I would indulge. So, no shame on those in power, I guess.

Matthew: No, I guess not. Dammit! It would be nice to have someone to point the finger at. Maybe just *give* the middle finger instead?

Michael: Maybe even two middle fingers. That seems more than fair.

Matthew: Sure does. But it's gonna have to wait. I am pretty much out of everything: drink, smoke, and fire. And without these things, I'm getting pretty chilly. Plus, I've gotta piss now. So, let's pick this back up after a break.

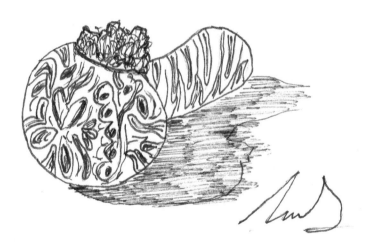

MIDNIGHT

Michael: So, I was thinking that we need to plant a new piss-tree. This grass at my mother-in-law's—while absorbent—doesn't have the gravitas I've grown accustomed to. I want something that I can nurture with my urine, something that will grow strong and virile. Should we go with another pine?

Matthew: Initially, I'm inclined to think as long as I've got enough whiskey and weed in front of me, along with a hot fire a mere yard away, I'm good with whatever. However, maybe we should switch it up like the Hobbits did after Sam brought back the Mallorn nut from Lothlórien. Not that our new tree has to be thought of as an upgrade or anything; it's just different. And different is okay. Sometimes in life, you just have to keep the memory of that which has since faded, and make new memories with something else entirely. So, perhaps a mighty oak would be apropos? Or, even a small grove of white birch trees? I've always loved white birches.

Michael: I suppose that it doesn't matter what kind of tree it is. It's about what it represents. It's the spot that we go to relieve ourselves after drinking and living it up—that's the memory I have. I have *especially* fond memories of chilly evenings when the stars are bright. And honestly, I'm not a huge fan of pine trees, so a sturdy oak sounds good to me.

Matthew: Right you are. Life happens. Then death comes. Then new life springs up from the ground. It's the circle of life, ya know? I learned that from *The Lion King*. And so, what our new Shire will represent is just that: new life that has sprung up from the ashes—quite literally! It will never replace what was lost, but it should help make the memories of old more palatable, rather than merely bitter.

Michael: I've never been *too* bitter about the fire. It's been an inconvenience, obviously. I've been sad. But I've never been *that* bitter, because, as I've said before, other than losing material things I haven't lost much. I still have my family and my friends and my livelihood. I got insurance money. Paradise will never be quite the same again, I fear, but in an uncanny kind of way, I've been more grateful than I was pre-fire. Being on my property, or my parents' property, floods me with wonderful memories of the past, of my childhood. Everything is packed with meaning, if you catch my drift.

Matthew: I do. And sometimes loss nudges us toward a posture of gratitude, which is, I suppose, a good thing. Being grateful for what you have is crucial to being happy in life. It would be nice if we didn't have to experience the pain of loss in order to be appreciative of what we've got, and perhaps it's not entirely necessary; it just seems that gratitude manifests when we reflect on what once was. Perhaps being more enlightened is about recognizing what we have in this beautiful, present moment, without needing any reminders from the past.

Michael: It helps to remember that life isn't a given; existence isn't a given. I am not owed my own existence, and actually, there's no reason I can see that anything should exist. Seen from this perspective, life becomes quite miraculous, and, I'll use this word again, uncanny.

Matthew: It is pretty odd, isn't it? That this sort of life, or any life for that matter, actually exists. I'm not sure what to make of it sometimes. But maybe that's the point. Maybe we aren't supposed to make anything of it and simply enjoy it. I'm not sure how you can always do that in the midst of forest fires, pandemics, or police brutality, but if I figure that out, I'll let you know. Perhaps it's like you've always said; human beings need an adventure *and* a home. The thing about an adventure, though, is that you're not ever 100% sure you'll make it home. That's what makes it an actual adventure, but it's also what makes it somewhat terrifying.

Michael: To be clear, death should be expected on this adventure we call life, for sure, but then we return home. We should always be secure in the knowledge that we're never in danger of obliteration or eternal conscious torment. Life is adventure; death is the return home to safety.

Matthew: Given our neurotic anxiety and fear of death, that seems counter-intuitive, on the surface at least. But I think you're actually correct, that death is really just a waking up from a bizarre dream. I have no evidence of that outside of some anecdotes I've heard from others (Mary-Anne Rabe, for one), but it seems to ring true in my gut. I feel as if we're going to wake up

121

from this thing called life and swear it was real, which in a way it is, but it won't be quite as real as what's on the other side. So, yeah, an adventure *and* a home. This is the adventure, but home always awaits. So far as I'm aware, that's true for all of us. In other words, we all die—or wake up, if that's how you want to think of it.

Michael: I hope it's not the other way around. I hope we don't wake up to a greater, more harrowing adventure. I'm getting too tired for this shit and I could use some downtime in my underground mansion in the Shire, smoking bowl after bowl of the Southfarthing's finest. Give me a thousand years or so to recoup and I might be up for a stroll to Rivendell, but I can't promise anything.

Matthew: That's how I feel, too. I'm ready to relax, enjoy a bowl, and work the garden. It's really the only work I want to do these days. Not that I'm lazy; it's just that I'm tired. Spiritually tired. And I'm in the opposite place from Bilbo. He needed a long holiday *away* from the Shire. I need one *in* the Shire. I feel like I've been running all over Middle Earth for too long, and what I really need are rolling hills, fertile soil, and a comfy hole in the ground. And, of course, pipe weed. Lots and lots of pipe weed.

Michael: I hope I haven't been stupid enough to find myself weed-poor. I'd better wake up from this life to hundreds and hundreds of different strains, enough so there's a different one for every conceivable situation. I want an Indica for every night of the week, and a Sativa with my morning coffee. I want one just for my birthday—if that's still a thing—and one just for

Christmas. I want one for the time I'll dunk over Karl Malone, with my balls gently grazing his afro.

Matthew: If heaven in this life is having that kind of abundance, then it has to be true come the next one. I can't think of a more heavenly existence than what you just explained, except for the Malone reference. I've never been a big basketball guy, so to each their own, I suppose. It would be pretty funny to watch a white guy dunk on a Black guy for once, though. All kidding aside, do you think what we experience after we die—taking reincarnation out of the equation for a second—will be similar in kind to this life? That is, do you think we'll eat and drink and smoke and have sex and ride dirt bikes? Or, do you think we'll just be in our pews, singing songs about Jesus until we're blue in the face? God, please tell me it's not the latter.

Michael: I think the pews will be there for those who want 'em. I don't imagine I'll be conversing with those people for a while, though. Like I said, I'm gonna be hanging out at my Shire-pad for a good millennium or two, then I'll probably take my dirt bike up into the mountains and live off the land for a bit. I think I'm really gonna embrace the hermit lifestyle, with the internet, of course—I'll be a hermit, not a peasant. It sounds too good to be true, but I don't know how else to interpret the phrase, "new heavens and new earth."

Matthew: Maybe it only sounds too good to be true because we're not yet there. We're in process. I have no idea what things will actually be like after we die, or when the new heavens collide with the new earth—which, so far as I understand things, is really just this earth restored—but I can only imagine it'll be like what you just said. We'll be in perfect union with nature. Our gardens will be manicured but perhaps not too much. Things will be wild yet tame. Crops will be shared should you choose to be in close enough proximity to do so. If you don't, maybe you'll be like Radagast the Brown—a hermit living a solitary life on the western eaves of Mirkwood. Sorry, but I'll be happily living out my days in or around Hobbiton, tending to my crops, and making the occasional trip to Rivendell or Lórien.

Michael: That's okay. You do you, and I'll do me. Living in eternity, the amount of time spent together and the interval between times spent together don't seem to matter. I'll see you when I see you, and eventually, that will add up to an infinite amount of time spent together.

Matthew: I suppose that's correct. Of course, it's all just speculative. It's fun to speculate though, so long as we don't let it distract us from this beautiful present moment we have right now. As intense and crazy as this adventure called life can be, it does have its place in the grand scheme of things. I can't really believe otherwise. It's just not, as I've heard you put it, a high-stakes game of the highest order, like the Evangelicals tend to suggest.

Michael: That's correct.

Matthew: So, when it's all said and done, like you just said, "Do you, Boo, and I'll do me." There is no "should." It's more about doing what you want to do in life, and I can't help but think that extends to after the point of death. I have no reason to believe otherwise.

Michael: It's an idea that seems to be a natural byproduct of a God that is sovereign and good. A good God wants his creation to flourish, and I can't think of a situation more conducive to flourishing, than one where people are never rushed for time to accomplish all their heart's desires. Any situation that puts the narrative of the soul to an end is infinitely tragic; it renders the entire narrative pointless. Why do anything if at some point nothing will be remembered or learned from?

Matthew: That's why I've argued how annihilationism is not only nihilistic but is really just a different version of eternal conscious torment. Not only is it pointless for people to be snuffed out of existence, but for those who continue on, it's pure suffering. Every lovely memory of the one annihilated would turn into a horror show. And no, a frontal lobotomy or Men-in-Black-style memory wipe doesn't help the situation. That's a sorry excuse of an answer to the problem, if you ask me, and not really worthy of a response.

Michael: No, I don't think God plays games like that. He lets the situation, whatever that may be, stand on its own without comment. If it's a bad situation, it remains bad until it is genuinely fixed.

Matthew: And fixed it shall be. What other options are there? Like you've said, God is sovereign *and* good, not good but lacking sovereignty, like the Arminians say or sovereign but lacking goodness like the Calvinists argue. God is both good and sovereign like the Universalists rightly assert. Anything less turns this whole thing into a tragedy, which you can believe if you want.

125

But I can't. While logically possible, I suppose, it's simply not something I can will myself to believe in; nor would I want to.

Michael: Given that Universalism and worldviews of similar ilk are more complete, more coherent, and more cohesive than other available options, I'm not sure choosing any of the other available options is actually logical. If Arminianism is your only option, sure, it has its own sort of internal logic. But, to my mind, it doesn't make much sense to choose Arminianism or Calvinism over Universalism.

Matthew: Both Arminianism and Calvinism have their own internal logic, and both claim to base their premises and conclusions on so-called "biblical truths," but every Christian seems to say that. For me, I just can't affirm all the premises of either camp. Their internal logic works, I guess, but their premises are, to put it mildly, a stretch. Much of it rests on a certain theory of scriptural inspiration (infallibility or inerrancy) and then builds from there. But why should I affirm this premise? What evidence is there for such a theory? Not much, if you ask me.

Michael: I suppose you might choose Arminianism or Calvinism for emotional reasons, say, for the satisfaction of watching your enemies burn. Do I really want to do the hard work of reconciling with my enemies? Heavens no. That sounds awful. It would be much easier if they just went bye-bye. However, anecdotally, I've found that the associated cognitive dissonance involved in accepting these theories is too much to handle, and once you experience the harmony of Universalism, you can never go back.

Matthew: Right you are. Once you experience the healing that goes along with a belief system such as Universalism—whether Christological, pluralistic, or otherwise—you really can't go back. At least, I don't know why you would ever want to. As difficult a notion as it is to have to reconcile with people you may not like, the beauty of Universalism stands on its own two feet. But you won't really know this unless you experience it. Like anything in life, to truly know something is to experience it. That's why Universalists always face some pretty asinine questions from people who have never lived as one. They haven't experienced this worldview so they look pretty ignorant when they try to press us on things. You know what I mean?

Michael: I do. I think that's because they have it exactly opposite: They trust the Bible over their experiences. They can't trust their feelings or what their heart is telling them because neither lines up with what they *think* the Bible is saying. Things get brushed aside as fairy tale dreams—as if that's a bad thing—when in fact reality is much closer to a fairy tale.

Matthew: It's certainly closer to a fairy tale than a horror film. With how many Christians talk about "difficult biblical truths," you'd think they were reading from a Clive Barker story. Honestly, I've never understood that dig—that Universalism is nothing more than a fairy tale. What's wrong with fairy tales? What's wrong with a happy ending? What's wrong with having hope that in the end all will be well? Why do we need the human story to end in tragedy for most who have ever lived? I ask these rhetorically, of course.

Michael: There's nothing wrong with a fairy tale, and I think that's what makes some people wary. Happy endings are too good to be true, and don't really happen in this life. But death in this life isn't the end of the story.

Matthew: If it were, then Paul would have been an idiot to mock it. "Death, where is your sting?" "Right here, buddy!" You're right, though; death is not the end of the story. It's an event in the story, but it's only the penultimate event. "Now" is perpetual. And after the event we call death, we will assuredly still be in the now. Why that wouldn't be anything but pure being, consciousness, and bliss—*satchitananda*—I have no idea.

Michael: Ah yes, satchitananda—the perfect description of God and a perfect note to end the evening on. Now, scram. I'm tired.

Matthew: Peace.

Winter

··· 10 ···
TWILIGHT

Matthew: Well, here we are, getting near the end. Not the end of our bonfire sessions as such, but the end of this current endeavor. I'm not as sad as I thought I might be, however. More excited than anything. Not excited to stop chatting with you—that will never happen—but just excited to wrap this up and see what's next for us and our journeys together through life.

Michael: It's okay, you can admit it: I'd get tired of talking with me, too. Maybe in its place, our next adventure should involve gardening. Or hiking.

Matthew: Gardening is always good. We witnessed the destruction of our little slice of permaculture heaven when the Camp Fire torched our town, so it's probably time to put our hands back in the dirt and see what we can again conjure up. I miss our peaches, and the giant batches of salsa we would make. And do you recall how ridiculously delicious those watermelons were? I never knew how good watermelon could taste until we sliced into one of ours. So, yeah, let's get back to cultivating the earth alongside cultivating our friendly bonfire chats.

Michael: I agree. Let's get back to the basics. Don't get me wrong, I enjoy creating content—writing and podcasting—but it seems like those should be extras, not replacements for bonfire chats and gardening. Sometimes life gets in the way (the Camp Fire, for example) and you have no choice but to abandon the basics. But dammit, as soon as my house is finished in Paradise, we're gonna have one of the biggest, most responsibly managed bonfires ever!

Matthew: Replete with red wine and something to roast over the fire, of course.

Michael: No doubt.

Matthew: It's just so fitting that these bonfire chats have been analogized with the seasons. We started with Spring because that's when things burst into life, and now we are in Winter, a season of death, where we are putting to bed this little project of ours. But, as time goes on, this will only lead back to Spring, where we will once again get our gardening hands dirty. That's just the circle of life. Things come and go. Projects live and die. The only thing that remains the same is the fact that things always change.

Michael: Yep. Things depart but they return again, albeit slightly altered. It seems to be a wonderful system for combating boredom. I tend to get a little tired of winter towards the beginning of March, even though it might be my favorite season. But give it three seasons and I'm excited for winter again.

Matthew: Like you've said many times before, people tend to need an adventure and a home. Perhaps the changing of the seasons—the changing of life's seasons—is all a part of that. I need some heat, days spent on a river or lake or out in the garden harvesting veggies, but even more than that, I need the cool chill of fall or winter, curled up near a fire with a good book or Netflix comedy special. To complete the analogy, we needed to jump into the adventure of writing these booklets, but now we need to head home and prepare the garden. Again, it seems everything goes in cycles. First, you spring to life. Summer brings adventure. Fall is where you slow down, reflect, and prepare for winter. And finally, winter brings stillness and death. It's all so hauntingly beautiful, really.

Michael: That makes sense to me. The adventure is the changing of the seasons; coming full circle is returning home. Or something like that. It seems that time does heal all wounds, including the wound of boredom.

Matthew: Time... and reconciliation. Complete reconciliation. Apokatastasis. It's funny that that word—apokatastasis—is in the very Scriptures Christians seem to worship, and yet they still scoff at the notion of a total and utter restoration of the human experience. I know you don't really dabble in the Bible all too much anymore, but it's right there, clear as day, in Acts 3:21. It literally says that God will restore everything. How they don't *see* this? I'm not sure.

Michael: I'm not sure either, and I've long since stopped caring to understand—not my problem. I'm a selfish bastard, remember? I said as much in the Autumn Session. The only thing I care about is that *I* have it figured out, that *my* soul is at relative peace. I also like that you obviously have it figured out. Actually, let me restate: I only care that me and my people (friends and family) have it together and that honestly seems to be the case.

But you know as well as I do: They're cherry-picking the Bible. You taught me a while ago that everyone cherry-picks, even us Universalists. We're just the only ones who know how to do it correctly.

Matthew: Yes. Everyone cherry-picks, including Jesus. That blows Evangelicals' minds every time you tell them. Can you say #triggered?

Michael: Hashtag triggered! I remember it blowing my mind. Deconstruction is personal but still relatively predictable.

Matthew: It totally is. There are nuances and no one goes through a step-by-step, detailed process toward enlightenment, but there are certainly landmarks we all seem to recognize along the way. What seems to be the most common experience is the emotionality of it all. Typically, people who deconstruct their faith lose friends and family—even their entire church community—and are forced to ride that grief cycle all the way through 'til the end. This seems to happen no matter what tradition you come from.

Michael: Yes, again, I can confirm that experience. I didn't actually lose any friends, but we threw verbal abuse and hatred at each other for a bit. It pushed me out of the metaphorical door of the church that I was already straddling, even if the church didn't know it. I was upset for a solid decade.

Matthew: Same, except I did lose some friends over that shit. For whatever reason, certain people just can't handle having friends who aren't a part of their religious tribe. I'm sure I played my part in them walking away, but it's sort of like Kafka's *Metamorphosis* in that once you change forms, people kind of act as if you never existed. It's rather sad, but once you move on from that, it's okay. You make new friends who aren't so rigid. And that, my friend, is quite liberating.

Michael: That phenomena that you're talking about actually makes sense to me. While it always sucks to lose friends, I at least understand why it happens. C.S. Lewis talks about philia—or brotherly love—in *The Four Loves*. While erotic love focuses on the other person, Lewis explains how brotherly love is focused on a common interest. So, if you're a theologian like yourself, it makes sense that you would gravitate towards people of a similar mold. You can still be friendly with non-theologians, even when they express ludicrous theological views, but there likely isn't going to be a strong bond of friendship, unless of course, you're both passionate about something else as well. And people's interest can change over time, so friendships naturally peter out. It's kind of a dick move to pretend friends never existed, though. Not cool.

Matthew: It's a dick move but, in the words of everyone who doesn't have anything better to say at the moment, it is what it is. Life is short and can be an out-and-out bitch, so it's not going to be all that helpful pining over lost relationships. Best to just dust those feet off and move on. Plus, I've got Lyndsay and Elyse, and I've got you and a few other close friends. So, it's their loss.

Again, it's all cyclical. Me and my former friends went through all the seasons and ended in winter. But there's no reason things won't circle back around. As you mentioned in *Autumn*, we all have an infinite existence—assuming Universalism is correct—so no need to rush things. Blossoms bloom in their own time.

Michael: When it comes to friendships, I hope we reach a state of eternal—meaning forever—blooming. A hamster wheel of blooming and dying is something I don't want to think about. I don't need the state of my relationships to be "adventurous." Sure, every relationship has seasons of separation, but that doesn't need to imply animosity or a death of the blossoms for that matter.

Matthew: I, too, hope there is an end to the cycles—a *telos* if you will. If the bodhisattva has to put her own enlightenment off forever, for the sake of friends who continually come and go, then what's the point of it all? At some point, we all have to reach the finish line, right? Like we've talked about many times around the fire, we're tired—tired of the adventuring, tired of the struggle. So, perpetual rest, among friends who are there for the infinitely long term, seems rather nice.

Michael: I'm sure the planet is tired as well, and ready for an eternal break—tired of us, that is. It would be doing just fine on its own if perhaps a little unkempt. Humans were supposed to be stewards of the earth, but apparently white people were too stupid and illiterate and unable to read the message.

Matthew: And too selfish. God, aren't we selfish! Imagine if we could all work cooperatively instead of competitively? We certainly have an abundantly plentiful planet, if only we put the right systems in place. It's a shame we act as if we have to hoard everything for ourselves. That's one reason I think capitalism is kind of shit: It requires infinite resources and breeds unhealthy competition. That's my opinion, anyway, one not likely to be embraced by most Americans.

Michael: Was it Shane Claiborne who said that there's enough for everyone's need but not everyone's greed? I don't get the impression that rich people are generally happier than the middle class. Surely planet Earth has enough resources for everyone to be middle class. The wealth gap we have in this country is frankly disgusting.

Matthew: Shane tweeted it, Gandhi said it, and I believe it. There's no reason why large swaths of the world's population have to starve, or not have access to clean water, or not have a decent roof over their heads. There will always be outliers—those who are hellbent on being complete fuck-ups—but the fact that so many people are living in squalor is a testament to systemic human failings. I mean, for Christ's sake! What do people need with $116 billion? Like you just said, does that make you happier than a nurse or firefighter or social worker or janitor? Not likely. And sure, they may not have to clean up people's shit for a living but I'd rather clean up shit than be a piece of one myself.

Michael: Well said. Take it from me; cleaning up shit ain't that bad. Neither is vomit. In fact, there's satisfaction in making the world sparkle. I can't do dog shit, however. For some reason, it instantly makes me gag.

Matthew: Hey, I appreciate the hell out of the janitor. And not just because you are one. Y'all make the world a more beautiful place, and without beauty, existence doesn't seem worth a good goddamn. We need more janitors in this world, alongside more nurses, firefighters, and social workers. More recycling professionals, highway cleanup crews, and oceanic professionals would be nice, too. But less corporate bigwigs making 500 times what their worker bees make would also be nice.

Michael: I don't have a problem with a huge wealth gap in and of itself, now that I think of it. It's the fact that there's not enough resources for everyone's greed. If there were enough resources for the poorest of us to be middle class, have at it you greedy bastards. It's still gross, but whatever. Like I said previously, I'm pretty sure they're no happier than me. It's a little bit like people who won't wear a mask during this COVID pandemic. Some people say, "It's my body and my right not to wear one." That's not the situation, though. Them not wearing a mask is possibly hurting my body, and you don't have that right.

Matthew: Yes, their greed is hurting others. And yes, while I have no issue with some semblance of income disparity—say, for example, Lebron James or Beyonce vs. the local barista—I do take issue with a CEO making an average of 500 times more than those who are directly responsible for the money being made, and then on top of that, watching the worker bees struggling to pay rent on time. But that's the situation we are in.

And if the Bible has taught me anything, it's that things are not gonna end well for us if we continue in that situation.

Michael: It's obviously not a sustainable business model. Seems that way to me, anyways, although I recognize many people are dumber than I am. People can only do the best with the faculties they're given, so there's no judgement. But you can't be afraid to ask for advice like, "Hey, am I cutting off the branch that I'm sitting on?" Or, "Am I stoking a worker's revolt?"

Matthew: That's the thing, though. Super smart people who own Fortune 500 companies *are* cutting off the branch they're sitting on, and yet they press on. Their greed is just so damn blinding that they can't help it. And when the sawblade finally breaks through to the other end, we're all gonna fall, them included. Rich cunts may get hit the hardest because they are sitting on much higher branches. We plebs are used to our lower-to-the-ground position.

Michael: It's a matter of greed and not intellectual faculties, for sure. Greed is sustainable for a little bit, and maybe these CEOs are just trying to get in and out. But greed is neither funny nor fun to talk about. Let's talk about how dumb Republicans are.

Matthew: Are they dumb or is it something else? Many are smart. Take Ben Shapiro, for instance. That dude probably has a high IQ, but is there anyone more insufferable than he? Maybe only Glenn Beck.

Michael: I actually don't think they're dumb. I only say it to be hurtful because they're super annoying. I have no doubt Ben Shapiro is smarter than I am. I even have no doubt that George W. Bush is smarter than I am.

Matthew: Ben may be smarter than you, and he's certainly smarmier. Bush, though? I don't know about that. I don't think he is really an idiot, but he did play one on TV. But you're pretty damn smart, and you don't have that god-awful accent. So, you've at least got that going for you.

Michael: I'll try to hide my erection as you say that. You're very smart to notice—that I'm smart, not my erection. But you were supposed to ask about Trump. I'd reply, "Trump is dumb as shit."

Matthew: Is he dumb or is he a master troll? I can't tell. Many of his supporters treat him like a cult leader, but are cult leaders dumb? Perhaps. I tend to believe he knows exactly what he's doing. He's playing people. He's found a large group of Lowest Common Denominators who are more than content to play the role of marionette. And so, here we are, fucked six ways from Sunday. I hope I'm wrong and I hope he's just an idiot, but I'm just not sure. Honestly, I can't keep up with the nonsense that is his presidency. It's like a bad B-movie. The script just doesn't make any damn sense and I don't have the energy to figure out the tangled mess of a story arch.

Michael: He's dumb, in the classical sense. He doesn't read, doesn't seem to know his history or geography, and I doubt he's very good at math. He does have a political intuition that might turn out to be effective, but I don't think he'd be able to tell you why it worked. That isn't necessarily a criticism, though—discursive thought is overrated in Western culture. Just because I can't tell you in detail how to ride a bike doesn't mean I don't know how, for example. The fact remains, however, that I'm not smart enough to use my words to explain how to ride a bike.

Matthew: Either way, I still like you. And really, isn't that what really matters? That Matthew Distefano likes you? That's what I tell myself, anyway.

Michael: I know that I myself like liking people. It seems to mostly work out.

Matthew: Speaking of liking people... I'd like you a lot more if you filled up my glass, and then we can pick this back up in a little bit.

DUSK

Matthew: Now that my glass is full, let me ask you this: Do you think that having these conversations matter? That is, do you think they actually help people? And is that even our goal? Obviously, we are having them for some reason, other than simply for fun.

Michael: I think these conversations *could* matter. Are they necessary, though? No. Anything important we say could be gotten from other sources. I think that what we say is important though, and I suppose who better to help those closest to us than ourselves, if we may be so bold. Ultimately though, I like these conversations because of the interaction and because I don't really know what I think until I put it to words. Obviously, I guess. So, they're helpful to *me*.

Matthew: Spoken like a true man of humility. It always seems the most secure among us let the work do the talking, and that those who have to always talk about how great their work is are probably making up for something—i.e., their true lack of quality. It reminds me of, well, you know who. And, not to mention, how in the Bible it's alleged that Moses talked about himself as the humblest man on earth (Numbers 12:3). Can you say *irony*?

Michael: You were talking about Trump, right? As I often repeat, there is such a thing as having a sober assessment of your own abilities. I'm pretty good at Call of Duty, for example. That's a real thing that can be verified with my kill-to-death ratio. Is being humble an ability? Let's pretend that it is. I'm a little concerned with the humbl*est* part, however. Surely, he wasn't well acquainted with everyone alive at the time. So, I have a hard time believing that Moses soberly assessed the situation.

Matthew: Well, yeah. And not to mention, no serious historical scholar thinks Moses wrote the Torah. I mean, there is a verse in Deuteronomy that describes his death, so take from that what you will. You're right, though; there is nothing wrong with acknowledging that you've got skills. Typically, you don't have to run your mouth about it, though. Unlike Trump. Great this. Tremendous that. How about just being a leader instead of waxing *un*poetic about it?

Michael: Or maybe wax unpoetically, but have the skills to back it up. That would be fine. Not great, but fine.

Matthew: I'd love to see more of us simply having an honest assessment of our own skills and talents. I know I'm a good writer, but I don't need to brag about how many books I've written, nor do I have to think I'm the greatest linguist in the history of humanity. A cunning linguist, but not the G.O.A.T. Again, if you're secure, you tend to do your thing and let the chips fall where they may.

Michael: Brace yourself for this: I'm not convinced everyone should be able to vote. I think it takes time, skill, and natural talent to understand politics well enough to not throw your vote away. It's painfully obvious that an ungodly amount of people on social media don't take the time to absorb news from reputable sources. I say this tentatively, not wanting to unduly suppress the vote, but I think you should have to take a test of some sort, something that measures your political literacy.

Matthew: People may freak out by your statement, but perhaps you're on to something. To my mind, voting isn't a natural good. Trump got voted president in 2016. Hitler was democratically elected, too. Which goes to show you that people can be shit-bags. Could Plato have been right? That the philosopher king (or queen) is a better option than the democratically elected leader? I don't know. At this point, the idea seems to at least have some semblance of merit.

Michael: You know where I stand on the matter. We're brought up in America to think that democracy is God's gift to the people, but given the right (or wrong) electorate, it's a mere step from straight-up anarchy. The evidence is currently right in front of us. Let me pose this rhetorical question: Would you rather have a wise autocrat or a democratically elected dipshit?

Matthew: I think you know my answer. But the United States was supposed to be the place where it doesn't really matter who the president is. Checks and balances, and all that. Yet here we are, reeling after having a leader who spent four years showing us just how inept he is. Now, let me ask you this: How the hell do we always come back to Trump?

Michael: We always come back to Trump because, as John Oliver notes, he's like one of his handshakes: He draws you in whether you like it or not. I don't wanna be drawn in, but I can't help it.

Matthew: Indeed, he does. I'm ready to shake free, though. Sadly, forty-some-odd percent of my fellow Americans aren't, and that scares me. So, back to your question—give me wisdom over idiocy, and I don't care if democracy is involved in the matter. Not. One. Iota. I mean, what's the point in democracy if you not only allow but encourage literal white supremacists to vote?

Michael: The point, I think, is that political or governmental structures are morally neutral. They're only as good as the people who wield them. Dictatorships can be a boon to the masses and democracies can commit endless atrocities.

Matthew: That's one thing I wish people understood. Whether a country is a democracy, a republic, communist or socialist, doesn't matter nearly as much as what that country is *actually* doing on their own shores and abroad. For decades, centuries even, this "great" nation has been democratic in its orientation, and yet has a track record of committing countless atrocities both here and overseas. The failed Drug War? Horrible. Racist. A disaster. The failed War on Terror? A human rights nightmare. Vietnam? A war we never should have been in. The genocide of the Native Americans? An utter tragedy. The kidnapping and subsequent enslavement of Black Africans? Well, you get the idea. We've done some pretty horrific shit, so it's sort of stupid for us to bemoan other forms of government so flippantly and eagerly.

Michael: You know, we watch the state-run media from countries like North Korea and we laugh at the propaganda. But how much of so-called American greatness has been mere propaganda? I'll admit that my knowledge of American history—and history in general—is poor, but my guess is that we've been lied to a fair amount.

Matthew: And worse than that. Joseph Goebbels, the notorious Nazi propagandist, was heavily influenced by Austrian-*American* Edward Bernays. You may not know who he is, but he is dubbed the "father of public relations,"[1] which, of course, is just a euphemism for "propaganda." So, in other words, we've been in the business of lying and deceiving the public for a long time. Not to be too distracting, but have you ever seen *Reefer Madness*? Although fucking hilarious, it's the most asinine bit of propaganda I've seen in my entire thirty-eight-year life and helped solidify the American public's negative view toward cannabis, one that is still intact today (in some circles, at least).

Michael: No, I've never seen *Reefer Madness*, but I'm aware of anti-weed hysteria, obviously. Like the poor, we're always gonna have the squares, the alt-right, the Trumpists. Do we try to empathize? Do we kill them with AIDS? I don't know, and it

....

1 "Edward Bernays, 'Father of Public Relations' and Leader in Opinion Making, Dies at 103." *The New York Times*. March 10, 1995.

makes my head spin. I literally don't know how someone can support Trump.

Matthew: Nor I. But they do. In droves. This is just the way of the world. We've supported tyrants throughout our history. For some reason, we like strongmen, until those strongmen start pushing us around, that is. Until that happens, though, we fall down and kiss the ground they walk on. When will we learn? Probably not anytime soon.

Michael: Maybe never. I don't know, man. I know that Biden has an FDR-sized plan to put this country on track, but our divisions are only getting deeper. Frankly, too many people are ignorant and unwilling to compromise and genuinely look at people across the aisle as enemies. I myself have a huge problem with conservatives, and I hate that about me. To me, it all sounds like a recipe for fascism.

Matthew: Something that would help the situation would be to admit that even if we disagree on politics or religion, there are things that can bring us together. We all have similarities. I bet there are conservatives out there who ride dirt-bikes, for example. As a culture, we just like to look at the divide instead of looking at what makes us all really, really similar. Why this is the case? I don't know for sure, but I'm well aware that it wasn't always quite like this. Not to this extent, anyway.

Michael: Most of the people I dirt-bike with are conservatives, in fact. I remember a time, before 2016, when I didn't politically judge people. I suppose you could point to Trump and 2016, or

Newt Gingrich, or Ronald Reagan, or Fox News, as reasons why people further segregated and separated—all conservative forces, by the way.

Matthew: Conservatives have worsened the chasm, for sure. But liberals have played their part, too. I've had a couple run-ins with them on social media. One time, back when Hilary Clinton was running for president, a liberal called me "alt-right" for criticizing her foreign policy and propensity toward war-mongering. I thought that was hilarious, given how socially liberal I am. Of course, that's just one example, and I *do* think conservatives have done more damage in this regard. Regardless, how do we heal? How does a society learn to get along and look past our differences and accept one another? How do we accept the diversity? How do we accept the uniqueness that is America?

Michael: Among other things, we have to accept that everyone wants what's best for the country. Progressives have to accept that not all fundamentals are bad, and conservatives have to accept that there is such a thing as progress, that nobody gets it right on the first try. Again, people need an adventure and they need a home. There are certain truths that we can always return home to, but there are also always gonna be truths that we have to adventure to.

Matthew: That seems pragmatic. I think what I'm most annoyed with is that we seem to be in a constant state of assuming the worst in those across the aisle from us. Like, progressives think all conservatives are hateful, racist rednecks, while conservatives think all progressives hate America. But the people who actually

149

fall into those categories are pretty few and far between. There must be a middle way, right?

Michael: Must there? Or, are we talking about the middle way between sense and nonsense? Are we eating only half the pile of shit instead of the whole thing? I haven't worked that out yet. I'm still toying with the idea that progressivism is a wholesome bowl of BBQ veggies, while conservatism is, well, a pile of shit. Because let's not pretend that progressives are against fundamental values like honesty, hard work, and human dignity. We're only against abolishing abortion because we know that prohibitions never work, for example. We don't take joy in ending human potential. Does that make sense?

Matthew: It makes sense to me, but try telling that to the staunchest conservative. Again, with so much black-and-white thinking out there, it's difficult to have any semblance of an adult conversation. That's the beauty of our Sessions here. They're so nuanced that many people these days will struggle with them, but maybe that's how we know we're on the right track. Progress is uncomfortable. It's an adventure. And while a home awaits, you don't come to appreciate home without the adventure. That was true for Samwise Gamgee at the end of *The Return of the King*, so it must be true for the rest of us, if you catch my meaning.

Michael: If you're meaning we should abandon the Bible for *The Lord of the Rings*, then I couldn't agree more!

Matthew: Well, if I'm being honest, *The Lord of the Rings* is a much more enjoyable read. And I relate to Tolkien's characters more than the biblical ones. However, who am I but a hellbound heretic, destined for the flames of Mt. Doom, or hell, or wherever else Christians think I'm going?

Michael: Despite its name, I've never taken Mt. Doom to be a place of punishment. But I'm not a "Lord of the Rings" nerd, as much as it pains me to say it. The Bible kinda beats you over the head with its message. *The Lord of the Rings* has just as profound a spiritual teaching, I think, and, like you, I actually care about the characters. I'm sorry, but I don't give a hoot about Paul. I realize that I care more about a fictional character, but there you have it.

Matthew: No, you're right. Mt. Doom isn't a place of punishment. I was just kidding. And I say that *as* an unabashed "Lord of the Rings" nerd. To your point about Paul and fictional characters: You need not apologize for caring more about fictional characters than real life ones who lived 2,000 years ago. Are we really expected to have enough emotional energy to literally care about everyone who ever lived? That's impossible if you ask me.

Michael: The joke being—if I may speak for you—that Evangelicals are stupid and have even less knowledge about *The Lord of the Rings* than I do, therefore making it plausible that they would misunderstand the meaning of Mt. Doom.

Now, if Paul fought a dragon, I might care about him more. His story is just tragically boring for today's culture.

Matthew: I gotta be honest: I like Paul. But to each their own, I suppose. The only problem I have with Paul is that you're right—Evangelicals are stupid—and they often misunderstand him. But that's probably a conversation for a different time, and definitely one for a different book. Right now, I need to fill my pipe back up. When I get back, we can chat through one more Session and call it a night. What do you say?

Michael: Piss off then.

Matthew: Hey now! I'll be right back. Fucking snowflake…

... 12 ...
MIDNIGHT

Matthew: You still pissy?

Michael: Sorry, it was my cancer acting up. Hey, did I tell you I have colon cancer?

Matthew: Um, yeah. I wasn't sure if you wanted to talk about it here, so I didn't say anything. But since you brought it up... what the fuck, man? How you gonna go and get cancer like that?

Michael: It was probably all the sugar, if I had to guess.

Matthew: Maybe. For real, though, how are you holding up? I know you always talk about how life is a combination of an adventure and a home, but this is a little much, no?

Michael: Well, I suppose this is where the rubber meets the road. This is when shit gets real. If Buddhism were ever to help a brother out, this would be the time. And it has. There have been times that I've been depressed and cried, thinking about the future, but mostly I've been in the present. I'm ok with looking at my stoma now, whereas before I was horrified.

Matthew: It's easy to wax poetic about being in the present, about not labelling things "good" or "bad," but when we're faced with some truly terrifying shit, things get real. I'm happy to hear that Buddhism helps you deal with life and the curveballs it has thrown you. And isn't that what our faith traditions *should* do? Shouldn't they be something that helps us in the moment? Something that helps us deal with the adventuring?

Michael: They should also help in the mundane times. Peace is nice and all, but it isn't very exciting, and sometimes it's hard not to feel bored. I think "Prince of Peace" is the most admirable title for Jesus, but I have to admit that I still don't get it. Not in my bones. I haven't learned how to experience peace in my flesh and just be happy with the sensation. And I think Buddhism is an aid to this goal. Is this the final goal of all sentient beings? To experience peace in the flesh?

Matthew: It seems that is the goal. Or, at least one of the goals— peace in everything we do. This life is an adventure, so it's probably not gonna happen all the time, but there is no reason we can't experience peace even in the midst of suffering. I say that tentatively, however, because I think it's also okay to not be at peace while suffering. Like, if you aren't okay with your cancer diagnosis, it's okay to not be okay. It's my wholehearted belief that you will be okay, though. Will it take multiple incarnations? Perhaps. I'm agnostic about all the ins and outs of our soul-journey.

Michael: As long as nobody gets obliterated, everything is fine. In this life, you get hurt and then you move on. You struggle, which isn't peaceful, and then things get better. We are the suffering servants. There's no reason for a soul to run out of chances to get it right. All that to say, everything is "okay" as long as souls are given the chance to make things right.

Matthew: I was just having a discussion with someone about this the other day. She asked me if everyone "makes it to heaven" in the end. I said that I believe so. Because if God truly is love, and truly has the type of power I believe God has, then why not? Would God ever give up on someone's soul simply because they are stubborn? Would I ever give up on my daughter if she went off the rails and became a total monster? Hell no! So, why should we ever suggest that hell is eternal? Why would we ever think annihilation is any sort of final answer to the problem of evil or suffering? Both "answers"—eternal hell and annihilation—are absurd. So, we're all gonna be fine.

Michael: There seems to be a lot of projection going on. People get tired of dealing with shit, so they assume that God also gets tired, and then eventually gives up. But that's why God invented the fucking "nap." Maybe he does get "tired." But then he "sleeps on it" and "wakes" with renewed energy. Why would this process ever end? What's the fuel that he would eventually run out of? But even given the answers to these rhetorical questions, I know that Trump supporters, for example, are stupid, but they're not *that* stupid. They might take a couple reincarnations to get it right, but not nearly an infinite amount.

Matthew: Maybe all of us need a couple reincarnations to get it right. Or, maybe there are people like me who get it right on the first try.

Michael: There are both types of people. There are the Distefanos and there are the Machugas.

Matthew: Let's not get it twisted: I *may* need a few more goes. As we've discussed before, I'd rather be done with the cycle of life and death, of course, but I wouldn't be surprised if a few more incarnations were needed to get me over the proverbial finish line. Or, perhaps we all wake up from this life and decide for ourselves whether we want to jump back in or not. Perhaps it's like a VR game, and if we don't wanna play any longer, we don't have to. I guess time will tell.

Michael: Or, maybe we get the option of taking as long of a break as we want. I don't like the idea of being reincarnated again either. But I say that while being tired. Maybe ten-thousand years of relaxation will make the idea of needing an adventure more appealing.

Matthew: That rings true in my gut. You've got a decent excuse for your exhaustion. I've never had cancer, but I could only imagine how tiring it would be. I'm tired, too, but for different reasons. Life is fairly draining, and I'm only thirty-eight. If I make it to, say, eighty, I could imagine being a real grumpy pain in the ass. So, yeah, I'm gonna need at least ten-thousand years of Shire-living before heading out on another adventure. I must admit, though: I'm really glad our adventures are being done together, even if they are tiring. I feel bad for people who don't have a fellow Hobbit to journey with.

Michael: For my own sanity, it's nice to know there's someone out there that basically sees the same world that I do. It's nice to have that confirmation. In a certain sense, parts of life have to be faced alone. Nobody can take away the inevitability of individual, physical pain, for example. But having someone to commiserate with helps, somehow, with enduring both physical and mental anguish.

Matthew: Agreed. No one knows about your subjective experience with suffering, but we all know what it means to suffer. And if Buddhism has taught me anything, it's that our job as bodhisattvas is to show compassion to all, attaining Buddhahood for the benefit of others. Not to be overly dramatic, but I must say that your enlightenment has really benefitted me in this way, so kudos to you for that.

Michael: Well, I'm happy and honored to have been some help. I lead a pretty small life, so it's encouraging to know that there's been some impact. I've stated before how impressed I am with your ability to get shit done. We seem to complement each other quite well.

Matthew: We most definitely do. And isn't it funny how when you first introduced me to Buddhism, I got a bit stressed out? Now, here I am, indebted to its tenets—indebted to you for having the guts to tell me all about it. Life is peculiar like that, isn't it? You go from bristling at an idea to completely embracing it, not some ten years later.

Michael: I've really raced through the heresies these past fifteen years. I can't remember the exact order, but I've ditched homophobia, biblical inerrancy, and deism. I've grown enamored with Eastern religions in general and meditation specifically. I've learned to trust my instincts and direct experience. I believe everyone will be saved. I'm even entertaining the idea that I'm God, for Christ's sake.

Matthew: So, in other words, it really was the kind of slippery slope our fundamentalist counterparts warned us about? Except instead of descending into a life of hell, you've found your place in the world and learned how to deal with life's bullshit. Sounds like heresy is the way to go, my friend.

Michael: The external circumstances of life have gotten more complicated and chaotic, but the reality of a peaceful rest at the end is more certain. Sounds like a fair trade to me.

Matthew: Plus, doesn't the belief and hope in that peaceful rest make dealing with the chaotic complications much easier? Knowing that even if the worst should happen—say, I drop dead midsentence—there is peace on the proverbial "other side." That gives me great comfort. It gives me great comfort knowing that yes, I may suffer, but that there is a finality to all suffering.

Michael: Sure. Sometimes I feel like hope is overrated. Sometimes I feel like hope for a better future steals from the genuine goodness of the present moment. I'm sick, yes, but there's also so much good, despite the bad. Friendship. Video games. Love. But if I had no hope for the ultimate future, that would destroy everything.

Matthew: That's what I'm trying to say. Hope for the ultimate future is a part of what makes shitty situations more palatable. It's not the only thing, but it seems to be a key ingredient. It's like, what makes a good risotto? A bunch of things—arborio rice, bouillon or stock, white wine, garlic, some veggies, etc. But without time and patience, you're gonna come up short. Same thing when it comes to our hope for the ultimate future. Without a universalistic ending, it's a bit of a fucked-up situation we're all in.

Michael: A toxic situation as well. I lived a good portion of life not having enough hope about the future. That sort of stress can't be healthy. Maybe it contributed to my cancer.

Matthew: It's possible, man. Stress does things to the body that we may not initially feel, but behind the scenes, it really adds up. And you don't really know how stressed you are until you get on the other side of it. Then, you look back and realize how clenched up you were. I wouldn't go so far as to say that the belief in something like eternal hell directly caused your cancer, but I can't rule it out either. I'm sure it played *some* part, though.

Michael: I'm gonna say that it did. I need something to blame. I need my pound of flesh, and I'd rather it not be mine. My beef is not with the enlightened forms of Christianity, but with the turd of a religion that I grew up with. I know we've shit all over fundamentalism in these conversations and I do feel a little

161

guilty about it because there are people I genuinely like who are still caught up in it, and I don't enjoy the thought of hurting their feelings. But good God, like Donald Trump and Trumpism in general, it has to go away.

Matthew: It does. And it is. Slowly. But some people are still holding onto it, white-knuckled and all. I feel bad for them, to be honest. Again, you don't know how much of a negative effect something like fundamentalism has on you until you are on the other side of it. Not all my days were tortured by the threat of eternal torment, but it was always lurking somewhere in the recesses of my mind. Now that I'm past that, it's crystal clear how detrimental that belief was.

Michael: Even though I'm not sure there is such a thing as wasting time, the time I've spent believing in eternal conscious torment was really just a waste of time. Whatever harm it did is now healed. But, think of all the Sunday mornings I could have spent watching cartoons, or playing Zelda, or huffing paint for that matter. I could have actually had full weekends—two full days off. Because there's no way I'd be going to church if I didn't believe in that kind of hell, other than being forced by my parents, of course. God-fucking-damnit!

Matthew: I think of all the time I wasted playing shit-music every Sunday, pretending I was having a good time so others could get their worship on. But it's whatever. I'm not gonna waste even more time bitching about it. I'm free. You're free. And, correct me if I'm wrong, but neither of us are going back any time soon. My only fear is that I'll one day be reincarnated into some conservative Evangelical family. That would be some shit, now wouldn't it?

Michael: That would be like the restaurant in Paradise that was rebuilt after a kitchen fire only to be burned down a year later in the Camp Fire—it would be so tragic that it's kind of funny. Maybe you have to do some Gandhi or Jesus-type shit to level-up out of conservativism in your next incarnation.

Matthew: I don't know. That sounds kinda cruel. Like we've talked about so many times, I'm tired. If that sort of irony is gonna be my fate, I'll need at least a thousand years between incarnations. Or, at least a different sort of personality. Because I'm way too iconoclastic to be trapped in religion again. That shit exhausts me.

Michael: True. I'm guessing that won't be your fate. You'll probably be that dude who spends his days sweeping the monastery.

Matthew: I could get used to that. Shire living, baby! Sweeping the steps. Getting my hands dirty in the garden. Pruning the fruit trees. That is my dream life, and I don't see why that wouldn't also be synonymous with heaven. I don't know, but maybe everyone's heaven looks a bit different, because I'm sure that would bore the hell out of some people. But not ya boy.

Michael: I'm pretty sure everyone's heaven will be different, and that it's up to everyone to build their own heaven. That's how I understand the "void." That's how I understand life in general. If

I had to follow instructions that wouldn't be life. As Alan Watts would put it, that would be a statue.

Matthew: Right. And who the hell wants to be a statue when they can be the real thing? Who the hell wants to be programmed like that? Life is what you make it, therefore heaven is what you make it. I have no conscious knowledge of anything other than this life, so if I had to guess, life on the proverbial "other side" would have to at least look somewhat similar to this one. Perhaps more spectacular, or more vivid, but in terms of what you actually do with your time, things would have to be similar.

Michael: There should be continuity between this life and the next. That only seems fair. Otherwise, what the hell are we doing here?

Finding your own way in life is more difficult, but ultimately, I think it's the only way. Every other way that isn't your own only leads to frustration, and frustration isn't sustainable.

Matthew: The beauty of being a human being is that when we find our own way, we realize that there are others who are going in the same direction. So, we partner up and walk the trail together, resting whenever it's needed. Meals can be shared together. Songs can be sung around the fire. Pipes can be smoked. And whiskey can be consumed. It's what you and I have had the luxury of doing, and I don't think I'd change it for the world.

Michael: For now, I'll let others do the singing, in public at least. My ancestors apparently had other priorities. But hell yeah, hook me up with some Buffalo Trace and let's relax like Jamaicans. That's part of my heaven.

Matthew: And sex. Copious amounts of sex. Fuck what the Christians have to say about the matter—that there won't be sex in heaven. There better be, or there's gonna be a lot of pent up assholes. Eternity is a long time, and I don't think my balls can handle a sexless infinity.

Michael: Sir, you make me blush. But for real, I had a C&MA pastor tell me that humans are sexual beings, and that heaven is just one big orgy. That's something I can do from behind. Wait. I mean get behind.

Matthew: If heaven is just one big orgy, people better start working out more and adding some fucking salads to their diets if they want me to be involved. Not that anyone does want me around, but still, let's be real. Americans gotta start putting in some effort, if you catch my meaning.

Michael: Yo, intermittent fasting. It works, and it's not that difficult. Burn calories. Life is about doing stuff. Be active and find your passion. Or, get colon cancer—there are options.

Matthew: Are you saying that your story is a cautionary tale?

Michael: Yes.

Matthew: Well, in that case, perhaps you really are a bodhisattva, using your enlightenment for the benefit of anyone who would dare to join us in these Sessions.

Michael: You're welcome. Welp, I'm beat, and I gotta empty my damned ostomy bag. Feel free to show yourself out.

Matthew: Will do. I'll make sure this fire dies out a little first. Catch you next time.

Michael: 'Night.

Matthew: 'Night.

THE BONFIRE SESSIONS

With rawness and vulnerability, as well as a large dose of salty language, the hosts of The Bonfire Sessions spend one night a week around a fire pit, chatting about the big ideas of life. Sometimes funny, sometimes profound, but always honest, the two hosts will be sure to challenge your heart, soul, and mind. So, pour your favorite drink and fill your long-stemmed pipe, and get ready for some high-quality fellowship.

www.thebonfiresessions.net

Many voices. One message.

Lightning Source UK Ltd.
Milton Keynes UK
UKHW020639210421
382364UK00010B/503